英汉对照世界名著文库

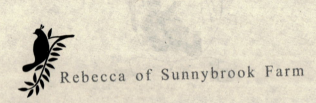

Rebecca of Sunnybrook Farm

Rebecca of Sunnybrook Farm

太阳溪农场的丽贝卡

[美] 威金 著

张帆 译

中国书店

图书在版编目(CIP)数据

太阳溪农场的丽贝卡 /(美) 威金(Wiggin,K.D.)著;张帆译.
—北京:中国书店,2007.2 （2012.12 重印）
（英汉对照世界名著文库. 第 6 辑）
ISBN 978−7−80663−217−8

Ⅰ.①太… Ⅱ.①威… ②张… Ⅲ.①英语−汉语−对照
读物 ②儿童文学−长篇小说−美国−现代 Ⅳ.①H319.4：I

中国版本图书馆 CIP 数据核字(2011)第 030902 号

英汉对照世界名著文库(第 6 辑) 太阳溪农场的丽贝卡

作　　者:	(美) 威金(Wiggin,K.D.)
译　　者:	张　帆
责任编辑:	杨　颖
装帧设计:	李艾红
美术编辑:	穆　红
文字编辑:	赵　晴

出版发行	中 国 书 店
地　　址:	北京市宣武区琉璃厂东街 115 号
邮　　编:	100050
经　　销:	全国新华书店
印　　刷:	北京一鑫印务有限责任公司
开　　本:	635mm × 940mm　1/16
版　　次:	2007 年 2 月第 1 版　2012 年 12 月第 2 次印刷
字　　数:	1247 千字
印　　张:	108
书　　号:	ISBN 978−7−80663−217−8
定　　价:	238.40 元 （全 8 册）

出版说明

为给广大英语爱好者提供一套便捷、有效地学习英语的理想读本,我们编辑出版了这套《英汉对照世界名著文库》系列丛书。其中收录了世界文学史上影响最大、价值最高、流传最广的经典名著,采用英汉对照的方式,旨在帮助广大英语爱好者通过读名著来学习英文。该丛书具有以下四个特点:

一、权威主编　质量一流

本丛书由著名翻译家宋兆霖先生担任主编,所选经典名著无论英文还是译文,都具有很高的文学艺术价值。我们试图通过这一努力,改变国内英汉对照名著良莠杂陈、令读者无所适从的现状。

二、一书两用　物超所值

名著是人类智慧的结晶,文辞优美,结构严谨,具有巨大的思想和艺术魅力。本丛书采用左英右汉的对照形式,帮助读者对照学习。使读者既可以阅读世界名著、陶冶情操、提高修养,又可以培养学习兴趣、提高英语读写能力,双重收获,效率倍增。

三、原汁英语　经典名著

本丛书除收录部分英、美等国作家的原著,对于非英语语言的名著,则由国内外知名的英语专家、学者以精准、流畅的英语重新编写,既保留了原著的精华,又使作品变得浅显易懂,从而避免了长篇名著的晦涩难懂。结合通俗、生动的译文,使读者能够准确地把握名著的精髓。

四、精编精释　理想读本

本丛书依照词汇量的多少及语法结构的难易程度,分为易、中、难三大部分,不同的读者既可以按不同的需求选择阅读,也可以由易到难,系统地学习。结合译作者精当的注释,以及相应的词汇表,帮助读者扫除阅读中的障碍,全面、深入、高效地阅读世界名著。

ABOUT THE AUTHOR

Kate Douglas Wiggin was born in Philadelphia, Pennsylvania, in 1856. At age 17, she moved to California to become an educator. Once there, she founded her own kindergarten and opened a training school for teachers. Wiggin continued to teach at the school that she founded until the late 1800s.

In 1903, wiggin published *Rebecca of Sunnybrook Farm*. It became an instant classic, and today it remains her most popular work. Other books by Wiggin include *The New Chronicles of Rebecca* (a follow-up to *Rebecca of Sunnybrook Farm*) and such lesser-konwn titles as *The Village Watch Tower* and *The Birds' Chrismas Carol*. Wiggin died in 1923.

关 于 作 者

凯特·道格拉斯·威金，1856年生于美国宾夕法尼亚州的费城。17岁的时候，她搬到加利福尼亚，成为一名教师。她曾在那里开设了一家自己的幼儿园和一所教师职业培训学校。威金一直在自己创立的学校任教，直到19世纪80年代末。

1903年，威金出版了《太阳溪农场的丽贝卡》，一时间成为经典，至今依然是她最畅销的著作。威金还创作了《新丽贝卡纪事》（《太阳溪农场的丽贝卡》的续本）。此外，还有不太为人所知的《乡村瞭望塔》和《鸟儿的圣诞颂歌》。威金于1923年去世。

CONTENTS

目 录

1

REBECCA ROWENA RANDAII

Mr. Jeremiah Cobb was hitching his horses to the *stagecoach*[1], thinking of the dusty road that lay between Maplewood and Riverboro, when a woman approached him.

"Is this the Riverboro stage?" she asked. When he nodded yes, the woman motioned to a young girl, who looked to be about eleven. "Could you take my daughter Rebecca to my sisters' house in Riverboro?" she asked. "Do you know Miranda and Jane Sawyer? They live in a brick house in town."

"I know them well," Mr. Cobb replied. "I live just down the road from that fine brick house of theirs. My name is Jeremiah Cobb, and I'm pleased to meet you, ma'am."

"Thank you, Mr. Cobb. My name's Aurelia Randall, and my girl Rebecca is going to Riverboro to live with her aunts

---

1. 本书正文中的斜体英文在文末词汇表中均有注释。——编者注

一

丽贝卡·罗威娜·兰德尔

杰里迈亚·科布先生一边把他的马套到公共马车上，一边想着从枫林到利佛保罗尘土飞扬的路况。这时，有一个妇女朝他走来。

"这是去利佛保罗的马车吗？"妇女问。见他点头表示肯定后，妇女向一个看上去十一岁左右的女孩招招手。"您能不能带我女儿丽贝卡去利佛保罗我姐姐家？"她问，"您认识米兰达·索耶和简·索耶吗？她们住在镇上的那幢砖房里。"

"我跟她们很熟。"科布先生说，"从她们那座漂亮的砖房往前走就到我家了。我叫杰里迈亚·科布，很高兴认识您，夫人。"

"谢谢您，科布先生。我叫奥里莉亚·兰德尔。我女儿丽贝卡正要去利佛保罗跟她姨妈住一段日子。索耶家两姐

for a while. My sisters, the Sawyers, are expecting her. Tell them that Aurelia Randall sends her daughter and her love to both of them."

"I'll deliver both your girl and the message," Mr. Cobb said as he swung up to his seat on the driver's box.

"Will you please keep an eye on Rebecca during the journey, Mr. Cobb?" Mrs. Randall asked hesitantly. "You see, she's too talkative for her own good. If she can get out anywhere, or even get people to take the coach with her, she'll try to do it."

"Oh, Mother, don't worry," Rebecca chimed in. "It isn't as if I haven't traveled before, you know."

"As if going to Wareham and staying overnight *constituted* traveling," Mrs. Randall laughed, shaking her head and rolling her eyes upward at Mr. Cobb.

"It did count as traveling. Mother!" Rebecca insisted. "It was leaving the farm, and carrying lunch in a basket, and taking a ride on the train — and we carried our *nightgowns*!"

"No need to tell the whole village about our nightgowns," Rebecca's mother said sternly. "Now, try not to get into any mischief. Sit quietly in the coach, so you'll look nice and neat when you get to Miranda's. Don't be any trouble to Mr. Cobb," Mrs. Randall scolded as she carefully counted out Rebecca's coach fare into the driver's hand.

妹是我的亲姐妹，她们正盼着她过去呢。请转告她们，奥里莉亚·兰德尔把她的女儿连同对姐妹的爱一起给她送过来了。"

"我会把您的女儿和口信一起带到的。"科布先生说着，纵身跃上驾驶座。

"科布先生，拜托您一路上照看丽贝卡行吗？"兰德尔夫人吞吞吐吐地请求，"您瞧，她太爱说话了。只要她能下车到外面，或者拉人与她一起坐车，她就会设法这么做的。"

"哦，妈妈，别担心，"丽贝卡插嘴说，"您知道，我以前又不是没有出过远门。"

"就好像去威尔汉姆住一个晚上也算是旅行。"兰德尔夫人摇摇头笑了起来，两眼注视着科布先生。

"妈妈，那确实算得上是一次旅行！"丽贝卡坚持说，"我们从农场出发，带上一篮子午餐，然后去坐火车——我们还带了睡衣呢！"

"没必要把我们的睡衣都告诉村里所有的人，"丽贝卡的妈妈严厉地说，"从现在开始，可别调皮捣蛋。乖乖地到马车上坐好，这样，你到米兰达姨妈家时才会看上去干净、漂亮。别给科布先生添麻烦。"兰德尔夫人一边训斥丽贝卡，一边把仔细数好的车费交到车夫手上。

"I know. Mother, I know! I won't be any trouble. All I want to say is ..." Rebecca called out as Mr. Cobb urged his horses into motion. "All I want to say is that it is indeed a journey when ..." she insisted, her head out the coach window, "it is in fact a Journey when you carry a nightgown!"

Mrs. Randall heaved a sigh as the word nightgown floated back, loud enough for all to hear. "Miranda and Jane will have their hands full with that young one," she said to herself as she climbed into her own wagon and turned the horses toward home, "but I hope they'll make something of my dear Rebecca."

"我知道了,妈妈,知道了!我不会捣乱的。我想说的是……"丽贝卡大叫起来,此时,科布先生甩动手里的缰绳,他的马开始上路了。"我想说的是,那真的是一次旅行,……"丽贝卡把头探出车窗,坚持道,"那真的是一次旅行,当你出门时带上睡衣!"

"睡衣"两个字随风飘了回来,声音大得所有人都能听见。兰德尔夫人深深地叹了口气。"米兰达和简将会围着这个小姑娘团团转。"她自言自语地说。与此同时,她坐上自己的运货马车,让马掉转身,起程回家。"不过,我希望她们能把我亲爱的丽贝卡培养成人。"

2

THE ROAD TO RIVERBORO

Jeremiah Cobb had just settled back and was allowing his mind to drift to thoughts of home when he heard a small voice above the rattle and *rumble* of carriage wheels. When he looked down from his driver's box, he could see Rebecca hanging out of the window as far as safety would allow. She was trying to get his attention by waving a fancy pink parasol in his direction.

"Excuse me, Mr. Cobb," she cried as he drew the horses to a halt. "Does it cost any more to ride up there on the box with you? It's so slippery and shiny down here that I rattle around on the seat until I'm black and blue. And the windows are so small that I can see only pieces of things."

Mr. Cobb waited until Rebecca's long speech ended, and then he boosted his talkative young passenger to a seat by his side on the box.

"Oh, this is ever so much better!" Rebecca exclaimed, ad-

二

前往利佛保罗的途中

杰里迈亚·科布先生刚在驾驶座上坐稳，满脑子都在想着家里面的事。这时，除了车轮发出的咔嗒声和轱辘声，他还听见一阵轻微的声音。于是，他从驾驶座上往下看，发现丽贝卡正探出车窗外，非常危险。她朝他挥舞手中那顶漂亮的粉色阳伞，想要引起他的注意。

"对不起，科布先生，"当他停下马车，丽贝卡大叫起来，"跟您一起坐在车厢上需要另外付钱吗？下面的车厢里太滑了，而且很刺眼，我坐在位子上来回颠簸，身上都要青一块紫一块了。车窗也太小，我只能看见一点点风景。"

科布先生等丽贝卡说完这一长串话，然后帮这个爱说话的小乘客坐到车厢上他旁边的位子。

"哇，没什么比这更棒的啦！"丽贝卡大叫起来。她戴

17

justing her sun bonnet and pulling at her darned white cotton gloves. "This is like traveling! Down in the coach, I felt like our setting hen when we shut her up in the chicken coop. I am a real passenger now. I hope we have a long, long way to go!"

"Well, Riverboro's about two hours away from here," Mr. Cobb replied in an obliging tone of voice.

"Only two hours!" Rebecca sighed. "Then we will arrive at approximately half past one. The children at home on the farm will have had their dinner. My elder sister, Hannah, will have cleared all the dishes, and Mother will have gone to help cousin Ann. Have you ever heard of Randall's Farm?"

"It's not the old Hobbs place, is it?" Mr. Cobb searched his memory of the region, scratching his head.

"No, it's just Randall's Farm. At least that's what Mother calls it. I call it Sunnybrook Farm."

"I guess it doesn't make much of a difference what you might call it, as long as you know where it is," Mr. Cobb remarked.

Rebecca turned the full light of her eyes upon her driver in reproach, as she answered, "Oh, don't say that. You sound just like everyone else! It absolutely does make a difference what one calls things! When I say Randall's Farm, do you see what it looks like?"

"No, I can't say that I do," Mr. Cobb replied uneasily.

好太阳帽，拉下那副有补丁的白色棉手套，"这就像在旅行！我觉得坐在下面的车厢里就像我家那只关在鸡笼里的母鸡。现在我是一名真正的乘客啦。真希望我们还有一段长长的路要走！"

"是啊，还有两个小时才能到利佛保罗。"科布先生亲切地回答。

"才两个小时啊！"丽贝卡叹了口气，"我们大概一点半可以到。那时，我家农场上的孩子们正要吃午饭。吃完饭，大姐汉纳清洗所有的碟子，妈妈就去帮安表姐干活。你有没有听过兰德尔农场？"

"该不会是老霍布斯的农场，是吗？"科布先生抓抓头皮，努力回想这个地方。

"不，它就是兰德尔农场。至少，妈妈是这么叫它的。我管它叫太阳溪农场。"

"只要你知道这个地方，不管怎么叫它都无所谓。"科布先生说。

丽贝卡两眼盯着车夫，流露出责备的眼神。她说："哦，别这么说。您的话就跟其他人一样！叫法不同当然会有差别！当我说兰德尔农场时，您能想象出它是什么样吗？"

"不，我不能。"科布先生不安地回答。

"But when I say Sunnybrook Farm, what do you think of?" Rebecca quizzed the old man.

Mr. Cobb felt like a fish removed from water and left gasping on the sand. Rebecca's eyes were searchlights that looked right through him in search of an imaginative answer. "I suppose there's a brook or stream somewhere nearby," hazarded Mr. Cobb — he simply was not a very imaginative person.

Rebecca looked disappointed but not quite disheartened with him. "That's not bad for a beginning," she said encouragingly. "There is a brook, but it is not just an ordinary stream. It has young trees and baby bushes on either side of it, for one thing. It's a shallow little chattering brook, with a white sandy bottom and lots of little shiny pebbles. Whenever there's a bit of sunshine to be had, the brook catches it, and, consequently, it's always full of sparkles, all day long.

"Are you hungry?" Rebecca continued, changing the subject. "I have some lunch, because Mother said that it would be a bad beginning to get to the brick house hungry and make Aunt Miranda give me something to eat first thing. It's a good day for growing crops and things, isn't it?"

"It is indeed," Mr. Cobb replied, amused by Rebecca's stream of chatter about so many different subjects at once. "It sure is hot today, though. Why don't you put up that pink parasol of yours to protect your head from the sun?"

"可是，当我说太阳溪农场时，您想到了什么呢？"丽贝卡追问赶车的老人。

此时，科布先生觉得自己就像离开水的鱼在沙滩上大口喘气。丽贝卡的眼睛像探照灯似的，看穿他正在寻找一个富于想象力的答案。"我猜农场附近有一条小溪或者河流。"科布先生大胆猜测——他并不是一个善于幻想的人。

丽贝卡看上去对他很失望，不过并没有泄气。"这个开头并不赖，"她鼓励他说，"农场上有一条小溪，那可不是普通的溪流。小溪两边长着小树和矮灌木。溪水潺潺流动，水很浅，可以看见溪底的白沙，还有许多闪闪发亮的鹅卵石。只要有一缕阳光，就能照到小溪上，所以小溪一整天都会泛着粼粼的波光。"

"您饿了吗？"丽贝卡换了个话题，继续说，"我带了午饭。妈妈说，要是我饿着肚子到砖房，一见面就让米兰达姨妈给我弄吃的，那会很失礼的。这么好的天气适合种庄稼或别的什么，对吧？"

"确实如此。"科布先生回答说，他被丽贝卡在短时间内喋喋不休地谈论这么多话题给逗乐了。"可是，今天天气实在太热。你为什么不打开那顶粉色的阳伞，好给你挡住太阳呢？"

"Oh, dear, no, I couldn't do that!" Rebecca *protested* in alarm. "I never put it up when the sun shines. It's too delicate. Pink fades awfully fast, you know. I only carry my parasol to church on cloudy Sundays. Sometimes the sun comes out all of a sudden, and I have a dreadful time trying to cover it up with my dress. My parasol is the dearest thing in life to me, but, oh, what a responsibility it is!"

It was beginning to dawn on Mr. Cobb that Rebecca was very different from most girls of her age. He took a second look at his young passenger — a look that she met with a childlike stare of friendly curiosity. The beige-colored calico of Rebecca's dress was faded, but very, very clean, and starched into stiff folds. From the little ruffle at the neck of the dress came a child's slender throat — long, brown, and thin. Rebecca's head seemed too small to bear the weight of the black braid that hung to her waist. She wore an odd little bonnet, trimmed with a twist of buff-colored ribbon and a cluster of black and orange porcupine quills that bristled over one ear, giving her the quaintest and most unusually striking appearance.

As to facial features, Rebecca's were not unusual, but she had the most extraordinary eyes. Under delicately arched brows, they glowed like two stars, their dancing light half-hidden in lustrous brown darkness. Their gaze was *brilliant* and mysterious. The way she looked at you gave you the impression that she was looking directly past the obvious to something beyond. Rebecca's eyes were like faith — the substance of things hoped for, the evidence of things not seen.

22

"哦，天哪，不！我可不能这么做！"丽贝卡警觉地反驳，"太阳照射的时候，我从来都不打开它，因为它太脆弱了。您知道，粉色非常容易褪色。只有在多云的星期天，我才撑着它去教堂。有时候，太阳冷不丁钻了出来，我只能急急忙忙用衣服把它遮起来。我的阳伞是我生活中最亲密的东西，可是，哦，照顾它真是麻烦啊！"

科布先生开始意识到，丽贝卡与同龄女孩相比显得多么与众不同。他再次打量这个小乘客——此时，丽贝卡也用孩子气的、善意而又好奇的眼神盯着他。她那身米色的棉裙有些褪色了，不过洗得非常干净，浆过的褶皱显得很整齐。那孩子细长的脖子从镶着花边的领口处露出来——又瘦又长，棕色。她扎了一根垂到腰间的黑色发辫，看上去她的脑袋似乎无力承受辫子的重量。她戴了顶奇怪的小帽子，帽沿上缠着一根米黄色的丝带，耳朵边直直地插着一簇黑黄相间的豪猪毛，这让她看上去特别古怪，与众不同。

说到长相，丽贝卡并不出众；不过她有一双最特别的眼睛。在两道弯弯的、精致的眉毛下，她的眼睛像两颗闪闪发亮的星星，若隐若现地散发出深褐色的光芒。她凝视的时候，眼神明亮又神秘。这让你觉得她能看穿隐藏在表面下的一切东西。丽贝卡的眼睛就像信念——渴望中的事物的依据，未见的事物的证明。

Mr. Cobb found himself unable to find the words he wanted when describing Rebecca to his wife that evening. When discussing the remarkable passenger he had brought to Riverboro that day, he could only stammer in admiration that Rebecca had eyes that could knock a person galley-west.

那天晚上，科布先生对妻子说起丽贝卡的时候，发现自己很难找到恰当的词来形容她。当他跟妻子谈论白天这位去利佛保罗的与众不同的乘客时，只能结结巴巴地表达对她的赞美之情，他说丽贝卡有一双能够洞察人心的眼睛。

3

THE BRICK HOUSE

"I didn't *volunteer* to be the making of just any child," Miranda Sawyer said as she read her sister Aurelia's letter one last time before Rebecca's arrival. "I supposed, of course, that Aurelia would send us the one we asked for, but it's just like her to palm off that wild young one on us."

"Aurelia needs Hannah at home to help her with the other children," Jane Sawyer reminded Miranda. "We said originally that Rebecca or even Jenny could come, in case Hannah was needed on the farm. Besides, Rebecca has had time to grow up and to mature."

"Or time to grow worse," Miranda mumbled irritably. "Moreover, if she makes as much work after her arrival as she has made this last week, we might as well give up hope of getting any rest ever again!"

"We've always kept a clean house, Rebecca or no Rebecca," Jane reminded her sister. "What I can't understand is why you've scrubbed and baked as you have all week for the arrival of this

三

姨妈家的砖房

"我可不是主动要抚养小孩的。"米兰达·索耶说。在丽贝卡到来之前，她最后读了一遍妹妹奥里莉亚的来信。"当然，我原以为奥里莉亚会把我们想要的那个孩子送过来；可是，她硬把那个野丫头塞给我们，这倒是像她的做法。"

"奥里莉亚需要汉纳在家帮助她照料其他孩子，"简·索耶提醒米兰达，"我们当时就说过，万一农场离不开汉纳，那么丽贝卡或者简妮也可以过来。而且丽贝卡还没完全长大，她会变得成熟懂事的。"

"或者说会变得更糟，"米兰达气鼓鼓地嘟囔着，"更何况，如果她来这儿之后还像上周那样惹出那么多事来，那我们从今以后别指望有片刻安宁了！"

"不管丽贝卡在不在，我们总是把房子打扫得干干净净，"简提醒她姐姐，"我搞不明白的是，在这个孩子来之前，你为什么整个星期都在洗洗擦擦、烤这烤那？你在沃森的店

one child. You've practically bought everything up at Watson's dry-goods store — cleaned him out entirely," Jane teased her elder sister.

"I've seen Aurelia's house and her farm and so have you. I've seen that batch of seven children wearing one another's clothes and never caring whether they had them on right-side out or not. That child will arrive here without clothes fit to wear — she'll have brought Hannah's old shoes, John's undershirts, and Mark's socks, most likely. I suppose she's never had a thimble on her finger and hasn't the slightest notion of how to sew. She'll learn, though — I'll see to that. I've bought a piece of unbleached muslin and a piece of brown gingham for her to make her own dresses. I'm sure she won't pick up after herself, and she's probably never even seen a feather duster. She'll be as hard to train in our ways as if she were a heathen from another country!" Miranda concluded in a harsh tone.

Just then, both women heard the rumble of the stagecoach outside the house. Mr. Cobb was bringing Rebecca right to their front door!

"Miranda Sawyer, you've got a real lively girl here," Mr. Cobb said in greeting as he helped Rebecca down from the coach. "I guess she'll be a first-rate company keeper."

Miranda shuddered openly at the adjective lively being

里购买所有的东西——都快把他的店铺搬空了。"简取笑她姐姐。

　　"我见过奥里莉亚的房子和她家的农场，你也见过的。我看见她那七个小孩身上的衣服都互相乱穿，从来不在意衣服是否穿反。那孩子来这儿没有合适的衣服可以穿——她很可能会穿着汉纳的旧鞋子、约翰的汗衫和马克的袜子。我估计她手指上从来没戴过顶针，而且一点儿都不会做针线活。可是，她来这儿之后要学做针线活——我会负责这件事。我已经买了一匹未漂白的平纹布和一匹棕色的方格布，让她给自己做衣服。我敢说，她不会无师自通，很可能连毛掸子都没见过。她就像个来自异乡的异教徒，很难用我们的方法驯化她。"米兰达用苛刻的语气作了总结。

　　正在这时，姐妹俩听见门外公共马车的车轮响起的轱辘声。科布先生带着丽贝卡来到了她们家大门口！

　　"米兰达·索耶，有个活泼的小姑娘来找你，"科布先生一边向她们致意，一边帮助丽贝卡下车，"我猜她会是一个非常好的陪伴。"

　　听到"活泼"这个形容词用在孩子身上，米兰达毫不掩

applied to a child — she believed firmly that children should be seen but not heard. "We're not much used to noise, Jane and I," she grumbled.

Mr. Cobb saw that he had said the wrong thing, but he was too unused to argument to explain himself. As he drove away, he tried to think of a safer word he might have used to describe his interesting young passenger.

"We'll take you up and show you your room, Rebecca," Miranda said. "Now, shut the mosquito-netting door tight behind you, to keep the flies out. It's not fly season yet, but I want you to start good habits right away here in the brick house. Take your bag along with you, so you won't have to make two trips. Always make your head save your heels. Wipe your feet on that braided rug. Put your parasol in the hall closet."

"Do you mind if I keep it in my room, please. Aunt Miranda?" Rebecca asked shyly. "It always seems safer to have it right here with me."

"There aren't any thieves hereabouts, and if there were, I'm certain that they wouldn't bother with taking your sunshade, but come along. Remember to always take the back stairs. We never use the front stairs because we don't want to get the carpet dirty. Your room is at the top of the stairs, here on the right. When you've washed your face and hands and

饰地打了个寒战——她坚信小孩应该被看到而不是被听到。也就是说，小孩子不应该多说话。"我和简都不习惯吵闹声。"她嘟囔着说。

科布先生发觉自己说错了话，可是他不习惯与别人争辩。当他赶车离开的时候，竭力想找一个更恰当的词，可以用来形容他那位有趣的小乘客。

"丽贝卡，我们带你上楼去看看你的房间。"米兰达说，"现在，把你身后的纱门关紧，别让苍蝇飞进来。虽然还不是苍蝇盛行的季节，不过我想让你从现在起在这座砖房里养成好习惯。随身带上你的行礼包，这样你就不必跑两趟了。以后也要处处长个心眼，别走冤枉路。在那块编织毯上擦擦鞋底，把你的阳伞挂在走廊的壁橱里。"

"米兰达姨妈，您介不介意我把阳伞放在卧室里？"丽贝卡怯生生地问，"把它带在身边总是更安全些。"

"这附近没有小偷；就算真有小偷，我敢说，他们也不会自找麻烦偷走你的阳伞，不过你可以带上来。记住，每次都从后面的楼梯上下楼。我们从来不用前面的楼梯，为的是不想把楼梯上的地毯弄脏。你的房间就在楼梯的尽头，靠右手边。等你洗完脸、刷完牙、梳过头，才可以下楼来。哎呀，"

brushed your hair, you can come back downstairs. "Say," Aunt Miranda said as she peered closely at her new charge, "haven't you got your dress on backwards?"

Rebecca drew her chin down and looked at the row of buttons running up and down the middle of her flat little chest. "Backwards? Oh, I see what you mean! With seven children back at the farm, Mother can't keep buttoning and unbuttoning everyone all the time — we all have to dress ourselves. We're always buttoned up in front at Sunnybrook Farm. Mira's only three, but she's buttoned up in front, too."

Miranda said nothing, but the look she gave Jane fully expressed her disapproval of the way the children were being raised. What on earth would they do with an unruly child like Rebecca!

米兰达姨妈紧紧地盯着这个刚来的需要她照料的孩子，问她："你的衣服没有穿反吗？"

丽贝卡低下头，看见衣服上那排纽扣歪歪扭扭地扣在平坦的胸前。"穿反？哦，我知道您说的什么意思啦！我们农场上有七个小孩，妈妈不可能给我们每个人系纽扣或解纽扣——我们都得自己穿衣服。在太阳溪农场，我们都是从前面扣扣子的。玛瑞安只有三岁，可是她也要自己扣前面的扣子。"

米兰达没有说话，不过她看了简一眼，眼神里充满着对这个孩子缺乏家教的失望之情。她们到底该怎么对待像丽贝卡这样不服管束的孩子呢？

4

SUNDAY THOUGHTS

One week after Rebecca had settled into her aunts' brick house, she wrote a letter to her mother.

Dear Mother,

I am safely here in Riverboro. My dress did not get very rumpled and Aunt Jane helped me to iron it. I like the stage-coach driver, Mr. Cobb, very much — he said that he and Mrs. Cobb might take me to Milltown to see the fair someday.

The brick house looks just the same as you had described it. The parlor is splendid and gives you chills when you look in the door. However, we are never allowed to sit down in the parlor, because we might ruin something. The furniture is elegant, too, but there are no comfortable places to sit down, except in the kitchen. I think Aunt Miranda hates me. Hannah was the one she wanted, because Hannah's more *obedient* and doesn't answer back so quickly. I'm doing the best I can to get along and to obey her, though.

四

星期天的随想

丽贝卡在姨妈家那幢砖房里住下来一个星期后，给妈妈写了封信。

亲爱的妈妈：

我已经平安到达利佛保罗。我的裙子没有弄得很皱，不过简姨妈还是帮我把它熨平了。我非常喜欢赶公共马车的车夫科布先生——他说将来有一天他和科布太太会带我去米尔顿城看看那里的集市。

这座砖房就像您以前跟我描绘的那样。客厅布置得相当豪华，当你从大门往里看的时候，会感到阵阵凉意。可是，姨妈从来不允许我们去客厅坐坐，生怕会弄坏什么东西。家具也非常高档，可是除了厨房，其他地方都没法让人舒舒服服地坐着。我觉得米兰达姨妈不喜欢我。其实汉纳才是她想要的孩子，因为汉纳比我更听话，也不会跟她顶嘴。不过，我正在尽最大努力与米兰达姨妈好好相处，并且听她的话。

I like the school. Miss Dearborn can answer more questions than the teacher back home, but she still can't manage to answer all the questions I ask. She says I ask so many questions she can't keep up with me! I am smarter than all of the girls except one, but not so smart as two of the boys. My new friend Emma Jane Perkins can add and subtract in her head like a streak of lightning! She is in the third reader, but she does not like stories in books. I am in the sixth reader, but just because I cannot say the seven *multiplication* table. Miss Dearborn has threatened to put me in the baby primer class with Elijah and Elisha Simpson — little twins who don't come to school as often as they should during the winter because they don't have warm coats and shoes.

I spend afternoons after homework sewing brown gingham dresses. Emma Jane and the Simpson children get to play house or run on logs in the river, but their mothers don't know they're doing it. Their mothers are afraid they will drown. Aunt Miranda is afraid I'll get my clothes all wet and dirty, so she will not let me go out with the other children very often. I can play from half past five until suppertime, and after supper for a little while, and on Saturday afternoons after my chores.

People are saying that it's going to be a good year for apples and hay, so maybe you'll be able to pay a little more on the *mortgage* to the farm. Miss Dearborn asked the class what the object of education was, and I said that the object of mine

我喜欢学校。与家里的老师相比，迪尔伯恩小姐能够回答我更多的问题，可是，她仍然没法回答我提出的全部问题。她说我的问题太多了，她没法跟上我！除了有一个女孩比我聪明外，这里其他女孩子都比不上我；另外，还有两个男孩子也比我聪明。我的新朋友爱玛·简·珀金能够心算加减法，而且速度快得像闪电一般！她在念第三个阅读班，可是她不喜欢课本上的故事。我在念第六个阅读班，但是，就因为我说不出七位乘法表，所以迪尔伯恩小姐威胁我，说要把我分到学前班，跟伊莱贾·辛普森和伊莱沙·辛普森一起——这对小双胞胎冬天经常不来上学，因为他们没有暖和的外套和鞋子。

每天下午做完家庭作业，我就开始缝制棕色方格裙。这个时候，爱玛·简和辛普森家的孩子开始玩过家家，或是在河边的木头上跑来跑去；不过，他们的妈妈都不知道自己的孩子在干什么。妈妈们担心他们会掉进河里。而米兰达姨妈却担心我会把衣服弄得又湿又脏，所以她不太让我跟其他孩子一起出去玩。不过我可以从下午五点半一直玩到吃晚饭，吃过晚饭还可以玩一小会儿，还有星期六下午做完家务后，我也能玩上一阵子。

人们都在说，今年是苹果和干草的丰收年。那么，您就可以多还掉些农场的抵押贷款了。迪尔伯恩小姐问班里的同学上学是为了什么，我说上学是为了能帮妈妈还清抵押贷款。不幸的是，迪尔伯恩小姐把我这番话说给米兰达姨妈

was to help my mother pay off the mortgage. Unfortunately, Miss Dearborn repeated what I had said to Aunt Miranda, probably because she thought it was an amusing thing to say, but it certainly was a bad idea. Now I have to sew an extra dress as punishment, because Aunt Miranda says that having a mortgage on a house is a disgrace and a blight to our family — rather like stealing or smallpox would be. She thinks that gossip will spread around Riverboro that the Sawyers have a sister who has mortgaged her farm.

I've written a poem for you about our mortgage:

Rise my soul, strain every nerve,
Thy mortgage to remove,
Gain thy mother's heartfelt thanks,
Thy family's grateful love.

You have to pronounce family's quickly, or it won't sound right.

Your loving daughter and friend,
Rebecca

P.S. Dear John — You remember when we tied the new dog in the barn and how he chewed on the rope and howled? I am just like him, only the brick house is the barn and I cannot bite Aunt Miranda because I must be grateful. Education is going to be the making of me, so I can help you pay

听，很可能她认为这是件非常好笑的事，可是这么做太不明智了。现在，我不得不额外缝制衣服作为惩罚，因为米兰达姨妈说，我们家有抵押贷款对整个家族来说是件不光彩的丑事——就像偷东西或感染天花一样。她认为，索耶家的姐妹有抵押贷款的事儿会传遍利佛保罗。

我写了一首诗歌送给您，是关于我们家的抵押贷款：

> 打起精神，绷紧神经，
> 誓要把您的贷款还清，
> 赢得妈妈衷心的感谢，
> 还有家人由衷的热爱。

您在念"家人"的时候发音要快些，否则听起来不太对劲。

爱您的女儿和朋友
丽贝卡

附注：亲爱的约翰——你还记得吗，我们把那条刚来的狗系在畜棚里的时候，它拼命地咬绳索，还不停地吠叫？我现在就跟它一样，这里的砖房就像畜棚；可是，我又不能咬米兰达姨妈，因为我得对她感恩图报。我现在所受的教育对我今后的发展有很大的帮助，所以等我们长大

off Mother's mortgage when we both grow up. Tell Mark he can have my paint box, but I'd like him to keep from using all the red, in case I come home again. I hope that you and Hannah aren't getting tired of doing my chores in addition to your own.

Your loving sister and friend,
Rebecca

后，我会帮助你还清妈妈的抵押贷款。告诉马克，他可以用我的颜料盒；不过，他最好别碰红颜料，万一我哪天回来还要用。我不在这段时间，你和汉纳的活儿又加重了，希望你们不会感到劳累。

爱你的妹妹和朋友

丽贝卡

5

A PINK GINGHAM DRESS

Rebecca tried and tried to like her Aunt Miranda, but she just couldn't seem to do anything right in her aunt's eyes. Rebecca was a *passionately* human child, with no desire to be the angel of the house. But she did have a sense of duty and the desire to be good — respectably, decently good. Whenever she fell below this self-imposed standard, she was *miserable*. She did not like to be under her aunt's roof, eating food, wearing clothes, and studying from books provided by her aunt, yet not like Miranda most of the time. She felt that this was wrong and mean of her. Whenever the feeling of guilt became too strong within her, she made another *desperate* effort to please the grim and difficult woman.

But how could Rebecca succeed when she was never quite herself in Aunt Miranda's presence? The hostile eyes, the sharp voice, the hard knotty fingers, the thin lips, the long silences — there was not a single feature of Rebecca's Aunt Miranda that appealed to her.

五
粉色的方格裙

丽贝卡千方百计想要喜欢上米兰达姨妈，可是，在姨妈眼里，丽贝卡没有一件事是做对的。丽贝卡是一个热情洋溢、有人情味的孩子，她不想成为这个家里的天使。可是，她觉得有责任并且渴望成为一个好孩子——规规矩矩、行为正派。一旦没有达到这个自定的标准，她就会苦恼万分。丽贝卡不喜欢寄宿在姨妈家，吃她们家的饭，穿她们买的衣服，甚至上学也是她们出的钱。大多数时候，丽贝卡并不喜欢米兰达姨妈。她觉得这么做对米兰达姨妈不公平而且很卑劣。一旦这种负罪感变得强烈起来，她就会采取另一种方式，拼命地讨好这位既严厉又难相处的妇人。

然而，只要在米兰达姨妈面前，丽贝卡就变得极不自然，那她又怎能讨姨妈欢心呢？米兰达姨妈那怀有敌意的眼神、尖厉的嗓音、僵硬而多节的手指、薄薄的嘴唇和长时间的沉默——没有一样能吸引丽贝卡。

Rebecca was not the only child who was uncomfortable around Miranda. The Simpson twins were so afraid of her that they could not be persuaded to come to the door of the brick house to visit, even when Miss Jane held gingerbread cookies for them in her outstretched hands.

What sunshine in a shady place was Aunt Jane to Rebecca! Aunt Jane, with her quiet voice, her understanding eyes, and her words of forgiveness and encouragement. She was such a help during those first difficult weeks, when Rebecca was trying to settle down to Miranda's rules. She did learn them, in part, but trying to mold herself to what seemed to her an extremely strict code of conduct made her feel much older than her years.

It is needless to say that Rebecca irritated her Aunt Miranda with every breath she drew. She continually started up the front stairs because it was the shortest route to her bedroom. She left the dipper on the shelf instead of hanging it over the water pail. She sat in the chair that the cat liked best. She did not close the screen door properly, letting flies into the house. She never stopped talking. She was always occupied with flowers, putting them in vases, pinning them on her dress, and sticking them in her hat.

Finally, and worst of all, Rebecca was the living reminder of her father, Lorenzo Randall. He had arrived in Riverboro twenty years before as a fancy-dance instructor, and man-

在米兰达姨妈身边,并非只有丽贝卡一个人觉得浑身不自在。辛普森家的双胞胎也很怕她,以至于没人能劝说他们去砖房做客,就算简小姐手里拿着姜饼给他们吃也没用。

在这个阴暗的家里,简姨妈对丽贝卡来说就像一道阳光!简姨妈有着温柔的嗓音和善解人意的眼神,她的话语又体贴又鼓舞人心。在刚开始那几个难熬的星期里,她尽力帮助丽贝卡适应米兰达姨妈定下的规矩。她确实把它们记在心上,并且尽量去适应对她来说过于严厉的规矩,这让她成熟了不少。

不用说,丽贝卡就连每次呼吸都会惹怒米兰达姨妈。丽贝卡仍然从前面的楼梯上楼,因为这是到她卧室最近的路线。她用完水勺把它放在架子上而不是挂在水桶上。她喜欢坐在猫咪最爱坐的椅子上。她总是忘了随手关上纱门,让苍蝇飞进屋里。她总是一刻不停地说话。她忙着把花摘下来插在花瓶里,或者别在衣服上,或者插在帽子上。

最后一点,也是最糟糕的地方,丽贝卡让姨妈不由地想起她爸爸洛伦佐·兰德尔。二十年前他曾来过利佛保罗。当时他还是一名出色的舞蹈教练,并且成功地俘获了年轻的奥

45

aged to sweep young Aurelia Sawyer off her feet and out of her senses. The foolish Aurelia had married for romance and love. She had stayed with her impractical, romantic husband even when it was clear that he couldn't manage to make a success of any profession it occurred to him to try.

Aurelia's share of the modest Sawyer property had been invested in one thing after another by the handsome but luck-less Lorenzo. He had managed to lose all of her money by the time he died of pneumonia during the winter Mira was born. His last investment had been a small, and more or less worthless, farm near Temperance, which now produced even less than was needed to pay the interest on the mortgage. To Miranda's disapproving mind, Rebecca looked exactly like Lorenzo — a black-haired beauty with eyes as big as cartwheels. She had also inherited his restless and overly in-telligent spirit, along with a head full of romantic notions. Now she was living under Miranda's roof as a continual re-minder of human impracticality and foolishness.

Miranda thought about these sad facts of human existence in the afternoons, when Rebecca took her sewing and sat be-side Jane in the kitchen. To Rebecca, the pieces of brown ging-ham — destined to be the only material for her dresses — were endless. She made hard work of sewing, broke the thread, dropped her thimble, and pricked her fingers. She could not match the checks on the gingham, made crooked and puck-ered seams, and caused her needles to squeak endlessly as they

里莉亚的心，令她失去理智。被浪漫和爱情冲昏了头的奥里莉亚嫁给了他。并且一直与这位不切实际的、浪漫的丈夫生活在一起，即便后来清楚她丈夫无论干哪行都没有出息也没有离开他。

奥里莉亚从索耶家继承的那笔遗产被英俊又不走运的洛伦佐接二连三地拿来投资。米拉出生的那年冬天，洛伦佐死于肺炎。那时，奥里莉亚的钱已经被他花光了。他最后一次把钱投资在汤普朗斯附近的一处农场，那个农场面积很小，而且也不怎么有利可图。现在，农场的产量还不够还清抵押贷款的利息。令米兰达失望的是，丽贝卡长得跟洛伦佐十分相像——他们都有一头漂亮的黑发，眼睛大得像车轮。丽贝卡还继承了他不安分、精力过剩和满脑子都是浪漫幻想的特征。现在，丽贝卡住在米兰达姨妈家，让人不时想起人类的无能和愚蠢。

通常下午，米兰达都在思考人类存在的悲哀现状。丽贝卡坐在厨房里，待在简姨妈身边做针线活。对丽贝卡来说，这几匹棕色方格布——是给她做衣服的唯一布料——永远都做不完。她做针线活费了好大劲，不是弄断了线，就是弄丢了顶针，或是不小心刺破手指。她没法通过姨妈的检查，线脚缝得歪歪扭扭，每次穿针引线都会发出吱吱声。幸好简姨

poked their way along a hem. Fortunately, Aunt Jane had the patience of a saint. Some small measure of skill was creeping into Rebecca's fingers — fingers that held pencil, paintbrush, and pen so cleverly at school, but remained clumsy with the dainty sewing needle at home.

When the second brown gingham dress was completed, Rebecca seized on what she thought would be an excellent opportunity to ask her Aunt Miranda if she could have another color for the next dress.

"I bought a whole bolt of the brown," said Miranda in a matter-of-fact tone. "That will give you two more dresses, with plenty of material left over for new sleeves and patches as you grow taller. It will be more economical this way."

"I know," Rebecca replied, "but Mr. Watson said that he will take back part of the material and let us have some pink and blue for the same price."

"You mean to say that you've already asked him if you could do that?" Aunt Miranda asked crossly, shocked once again at her niece's boldness at negotiating with her elders.

"Yes, ma'am, I did," Rebecca answered.
"It was not your place to do that."
"I was helping Emma Jane choose aprons when I thought to ask him. I didn't think that you would mind that much

妈有着圣人般的耐心。于是，丽贝卡学会了一些做针线活的小技巧——这双手在学校里拿铅笔、画笔和钢笔都很灵巧，可是，在家里拿针线时却显得那么笨拙。

等第二块棕色方格布缝制完后，丽贝卡抓住这个好时机，问米兰达姨妈下次能否给她换一种颜色的布料。

"我给你买了一整匹棕色棉布，"米兰达诚恳地说，"足够你做两套裙子；等你再长高一些，还可以用多余的布料做新的袖子，或者打补丁。这么做比较节省。"

"我知道，"丽贝卡回答，"可是，沃森先生说，他可以把剩下的布料收回去，然后以同样的价格卖给我们一些粉色和蓝色的布料。"

"你的意思是说，你早就问过他可不可以换布料啦？"米兰达生气地问。她对侄女胆敢与长辈讨价还价感到震惊。

"是的，夫人，我问过了。"丽贝卡回答。
"你无权这么做。"
"当时我正在帮爱玛·简挑围裙，我觉得可以问问沃森先生这事儿。我觉得您不会介意我到底用哪种颜色的布料缝

which color gingham I had. I'll keep the pink as nice and clean as the brown — you'll see! Mr. Watson said that it will wash well, without fading," Rebecca reasoned.

"I am only too convinced that Mr. Watson is a splendid judge of washing," Aunt Miranda said sarcastically. "I simply do not approve of children being rigged out in fancy colors. Jane, what do you think?"

"I think it would be all right to let Rebecca have one pink and one blue gingham," Jane replied gently, knowing that this was not the expected or desired answer to her elder sister's question. "A girl does get tired of sewing only one color. Besides, she'll look like a charity case if she is always wearing the same brown color with a white apron. The color brown doesn't suit her that well, either. She would look ever so much prettier in pink or blue!"

"Handsome is as handsome does," Aunt Miranda said drily. "There's no point in humoring that child about her looks. She is as vain as a peacock now — not that she has that much to be so vain about!"

"She's young and attracted to bright things!" Jane insisted. "I remember well enough how I felt at her age."

"You were young and extremely foolish at her age!"
"Yes, I was, and I thank my lucky stars for being that way.

衣服。我穿粉色的衣服会跟棕色的一样干净、漂亮——到时您就知道了！沃森先生说，粉色的方格布很容易洗，而且不会褪色。"丽贝卡据理力争。

"我当然知道沃森先生对布料的洗涤很在行，"米兰达姨妈讽刺地说，"我只是不赞成小孩子穿得过于艳丽。简，你怎么看？"

"我觉得，给丽贝卡一块粉色和一块蓝色的方格布没什么大不了。"简轻声回答，她知道这并不是姐姐想要的答案。"女孩子确实会对缝制一种颜色的布料感到厌倦。另外，假如她总是穿棕色的裙子，系白色的围裙，这会让她看上去像个慈善会里的孩子。而且，棕色也不太适合她。她穿粉色或蓝色的裙子会更漂亮！"

"行为漂亮才是真的漂亮，"米兰达姨妈冷冷地说，"没有必要迎合女孩子对外表的要求。她现在就像骄傲的孔雀——其实她没什么值得骄傲的！"

"她还小，容易被鲜亮的东西吸引！"简坚持说，"我记得很清楚，像她这么大的时候，我也喜欢鲜亮的东西。"

"你那时还小，而且傻透了！"
"是的，我确实很傻，为此我要感谢我的幸运星。如今，

I only wish I could figure out how to bring back some of that foolishness into my old age, to brighten my declining years in this house!"

That speech managed to silence Aunt Miranda for a while. Aunt Jane won for Rebecca the pink gingham. Jane also showed her niece how to make a pretty trimming of narrow, white linen tape, by folding it in pointed shapes and sewing it down very flat with neat little stitches. Rebecca sewed and basted the trim with renewed energy and enthusiasm, in an effort to get the dress finished as quickly as possible. Miranda decided not to say any more about the matter, but she was not happy about being defeated in her attempts to remain head of her household.

我活了一大把年纪，只希望知道如何把儿时的傻气重新找回来，照亮我在这座房子里度过的风烛残年。"

听完这番话，米兰达姨妈沉默了一会儿。最终，简姨妈为丽贝卡赢得了一块粉色的方格布。她还教侄女如何给裙摆缝上漂亮的白色亚麻花边，先把亚麻布按照指定的形状折起来，然后非常平整地缝好，针脚又细又整齐。丽贝卡重新振作精神、焕发热情，尽可能快地缝制裙子。对此，米兰达决定不再多说什么，可是，作为一家之主，她的威严受到了冒犯，这让她很不高兴。

6

THE FRIDAY RECITATION

Riverboro's schoolhouse stood on the crest of a hill, with rolling fields on one side, a stretch of woods on the other, and the river *glinting* in the distance. It had a flagpole on the side and two doors in front — one for boys and the other for girls. Not much besides the landscape was beautiful, however. All was bare and ugly and uncomfortable inside the school building. The villages along the river spent most of their tax money maintaining bridges and roads, so they had little left for schools.

Miss Dearborn's desk and chair stood on a platform, near the pot-bellied stove. Other furnishings were limited to a map of the United States, two blackboards, and wooden desks with benches for the students, who only numbered twenty in Rebecca's time. The seats were higher in the back of the room — the older and longer-legged students sat there. They were greatly envied, because they were both nearer to the windows and farther from the teacher than the rest of the students.

六

星期五的朗诵

　　丽贝卡的学校坐落在山顶上，一边是起伏的草场，另一边是绵延的树林，远处还有一条波光粼粼的河流。学校一侧竖着一根旗杆，前面有两扇大门——一扇给男孩子进出，另一扇给女孩子进出。然而，除了风景优美之外，其他的都不怎么样。学校里光秃秃的，十分难看，让人觉得不舒服。沿河的村民把大部分的税款都用来造桥修路，所以没什么钱资助学校。

　　迪尔伯恩小姐的桌子和椅子放在讲台上，靠近大肚皮的炉子。教室里仅有的布置就是一张美国地图、两块黑板，以及供学生用的木制课桌和长板凳。丽贝卡上学的时候教室里只有二十个人。后排的座位比前排的高一些——年纪大点、腿脚长些的学生坐后排。其他学生羡慕死他们了，因为那离窗口近，离老师又远。

One Friday each year was traditionally set aside for a public display of student progress. Rebecca had scarcely been at the school for a year when it was time for the next performance. Friday afternoon was always the time for the dialogues, songs, and recitations that made up the program of events. It cannot be said that the day was necessarily happy. Most of the children hated "speaking pieces," hated the burden of learning them by heart, and dreaded forgetting their lines midway through their speech. Miss Dearborn commonly went home with a headache, and did not leave her bed during the rest of the afternoon or evening.

Very few parents attended these exercises. Those who did sat nervously on a bench in front of the schoolroom. Beads of cold sweat pearled on their foreheads as they listened to the all-too-familiar halts and stammers of their desperate children. Sometimes an extremely young child who had forgotten his or her poem would cast himself or herself, bellowing, on his or her mother's chest. The child would be taken outside, where he or she was sometimes kissed and occasionally scolded. In either case, the potential for failure always added an extra dash of gloom and dread to the occasion.

Rebecca's presence at school, however, had somehow produced a new burst of enthusiasm for this year's Friday recital. She had taught Elijah and Elisha Simpson to recite a poem with such comical effect that they delighted themselves, the

学校每年都会在某个星期五安排一次公开汇演,让学生展现自己取得的进步。丽贝卡上学还不到一年,就迎来了第二年的公开汇演。星期五下午,总是安排对话、唱歌和朗诵表演等节目。这一天并不快乐。大多数学生讨厌"背诵诗文",不喜欢死记硬背,害怕说到一半忘词。每次结束后,迪尔伯恩小姐都是头痛地回到家,躺在床上休息一下午或者睡到晚上。

很少有家长参加这种汇演。那些坐在教室前排的家长也很紧张。听见自己的孩子熟悉的停顿和结巴时,他们的前额渗出豆大的汗珠。有时候,年幼的孩子背不出诗歌,就会一头扎进妈妈的怀里。这时,小孩子就会被带到外面,妈妈或者轻吻他/她,或者责骂他/她。不管结果如何,孩子们潜意识里害怕失败,这更增添了他们对那个时刻的恐惧。

然而,丽贝卡的到来为学校今年星期五的朗诵表演注入了一股新鲜的活力。她教伊莱贾·辛普森和伊莱沙·辛普森朗诵的诗有喜剧效果,结果把他们自己、老师,还有其他孩子都逗乐了。丽贝卡为口齿不清的苏珊写了一首幽默的诗

teacher, and the other children. Rebecca had composed for Susan, who lisped, a humorous poem in which Susan happily "impersonated" a lisping child. Rebecca had also volunteered to be Emma Jane's partner in a dialogue. Emma Jane was rather shy, but felt much more confident when supported by Rebecca's presence.

Miss Dearborn announced on Friday morning that the exercises promised to be so interesting that she had invited the doctor's wife, the minister's wife, two members of the school committee, and a few mothers to attend. She asked Huldah Meserve to decorate one of the blackboards and Rebecca to decorate the other. Huldah, who was the star artist of the school, chose to reproduce the map of North America. Rebecca preferred to draw things less realistically. Before the enchanted eyes of her classmates, there grew under her skillful fingers an American flag drawn in red, white, and blue chalk, with every star in its proper place, and every stripe fluttering in the breeze. Beside the flag appeared a figure of Columbia, copied from the top of a cigar box that held the crayons.

Miss Dearborn was very pleased. "I propose that we give Rebecca a big round of applause for such beautiful pictures — drawings of which the whole school may be proud!"

The children clapped heartily, and Dick Carter, leaping to his feet, waved his hat and gave a rousing cheer. Rebecca's

歌，苏珊很高兴地"模仿"一个口吃的孩子。丽贝卡还自告
奋勇与爱玛·简搭档表演对话。爱玛·简本来十分害羞，可
是，丽贝卡的参与让她信心倍增。

迪尔伯恩小姐在星期五早上宣布,这次汇演肯定十分有
趣,她已经邀请了医生的妻子、牧师的妻子、两名校董会成
员,还有几位母亲前来观看。她让胡尔达·梅泽夫负责装饰
一块黑板,吩咐丽贝卡装饰另一块。胡尔达是学校里的明星
艺术家,她选定在黑板上画一张北美洲地图。丽贝卡喜欢画
一些抽象的东西。在大家如痴如醉的注视下,丽贝卡的巧手
用红、白、蓝三色粉笔画了一面美国国旗,国旗上每颗星星
的位置都很准确,每段条纹都好似在迎风飘舞。在国旗旁
边,她又画了一个哥伦比亚的形状,这是丽贝卡从放粉笔的
雪茄盒盖上临摹下来的。

迪尔伯恩小姐非常满意。"我提议,大家为丽贝卡画的
这幅漂亮的图画热烈鼓掌——全校师生都会为这幅画感到
骄傲！"

孩子们热烈地鼓掌。迪克·卡特从座位上跳起来,挥舞
手中的帽子,发出一声欢呼。此时,丽贝卡满心欢喜,却又

heart leaped for Joy, and to her confusion, she felt tears rising in her eyes. She could hardly see her way back to her seat. She had never before been singled out for applause. She had never been praised in this fashion, never crowned as in this wonderful, *dazzling* moment. Rebecca took her seat in silence. Her heart was so full of grateful joy that she could hardly remember the words of her dialogue.

Miss Dearborn dismissed her students at close to noon, so that those who lived near enough could go home and change clothes. Emma Jane and Rebecca ran nearly every step of the way, bounding with excitement.

"Will your Aunt Miranda let you wear your best dress, or only your buff calico?" asked Emma Jane once they stopped to breathe at Rebecca's gate.

"I think I'll ask Aunt Jane," Rebecca replied. "Oh! If only my pink *gingham* were finished! I left Aunt Jane making the buttonholes this morning!"

"I'm going to ask my mother to let me wear her garnet ring," said Emma Jane. "It would look perfectly elegant flashing in the light when I point to your flag. Good-bye! Don't forget your lines! And don't wait for me to go back to school — I may get a ride."

热泪盈眶，她自己也不清楚为什么会这样。她几乎看不清回座位的路。她以前从来没有被老师点名鼓掌过，也没有像这样被表扬过，她从来没有体验过这种奇妙的、令人晕眩的时刻。丽贝卡默默地回到座位上。她内心充满了感激和喜悦之情，以至于差点忘了当时说过什么话。

快到中午的时候，迪尔伯恩小姐才下课，那些住在学校附近的学生可以趁这个时候回家换件衣服。爱玛·简和丽贝卡这一路上激动得又蹦又跳，几乎是跑回家的。

"你米兰达姨妈会让你穿上最好的衣服吗？还是只让你穿浅黄色的印花布衣？"她们在丽贝卡家门口停下来喘气，趁这个时候爱玛·简问丽贝卡。

"我想我会问一下简姨妈，"丽贝卡回答，"哦！要是我那件粉色的方格裙已经做好了，那该有多美啊！今天早上我出门的时候简姨妈在帮我做纽扣孔。"

"我要问妈妈借那只石榴子石戒指，"爱玛·简说，"当我戴着它指向你画的国旗时，它会在阳光下发出优美的光泽。再见！别忘了你的词儿！不用等我一起回学校了——我可能会搭便车。"

7

SHOW TIME!

Rebecca tried the side door to the brick house, but she found it locked. Fortunately, she knew where her aunts kept the key. She retrieved the key from under the front step and unlocked the door. When she entered the dining room, she found her lunch laid out on the table with a note from Aunt Jane saying that she and Aunt Miranda had gone to a meeting with Mrs. Robinson, and that they would not be back before supper.

Rebecca swallowed a piece of bread and butter, and flew up the forbidden front steps to her bedroom. On the bed lay the pink gingham dress finished by Aunt Jane's kind hands. Could she wear it without asking permission first? Did the occasion justify a new costume? Or would her aunts think that she ought to save the new dress for the next Sunday school concert?

"I'll wear it," Rebecca said to herself. "My aunts aren't here to ask, and perhaps they won't mind. It's only gingham, after

七
表演时刻！

丽贝卡想从边门进去，可是发现门被锁上了。幸亏她知道姨妈放钥匙的地方。她从前面台阶下找到钥匙，把门打开。她走进餐厅时，发现她的午饭放在桌上，旁边还有一张简姨妈留的字条。她说自己和米兰达姨妈去拜访鲁滨逊太太了，直到吃晚饭的时候才能回来。

丽贝卡吞了一片面包和黄油，然后飞快地从前面被禁的楼梯上去，冲进自己的卧室。床上放着那条粉色的方格裙，简姨妈的巧手已经把它做好了。她能否未经允许就穿上它呢？下午的场合是否值得穿新衣服呢？或者姨妈认为她应该把这件新衣服留到主日学校的下一次音乐会上穿？

"我这就穿上它，"丽贝卡自言自语地说，"姨妈不在家，来不及征得她们的同意，也许她们对此并不介意。它毕竟只

all, and the dress wouldn't be so terrific if it weren't new, and if it didn't have white tape trimming on it, and if it weren't pink." Rebecca slipped on the pretty new dress and managed to fasten all but the middle three buttons up the back — Emma Jane would have to help her with those. Then she changed her shoes and combed out her braids. She tied her wavy black hair into a single ponytail graced with a white ribbon.

Rebecca smiled at herself in the mirror. She felt ready to shine at her first recital. As she turned to leave her room, she spied her *cherished* pink sunshade. It was the perfect match for her dress, and her classmates had never seen it. It was too fancy for school, but she wouldn't take it into the schoolroom. She would wrap it in a piece of paper, just to show it, and then carry it coming back home.

Once Rebecca had finished wrapping her parasol, she glanced at the clock. Goodness! It was twenty minutes to one, and she would be late! She danced out the side door, pulled a pink rose from the bush at the gate, and covered the mile between the brick house and the school in an incredibly short time. She met Emma Jane, also breathless and magniflcently dressed, at the entrance to the schoolhouse.

"Rebecca Rowena Randall!" exclaimed Emma Jane excitedly. "You're as handsome as a picture!"
"Nonsense!" laughed Rebecca. "It's the pink gingham."
"You're not so good-looking every day," insisted Emma

是一条方格裙,假如它不是新的,没有镶着白色的花边,也不是粉色的,那它看上去就不会这么漂亮。"丽贝卡赶紧穿上这件漂亮的新衣服,想要扣上所有的纽扣;可是,后背中间有三颗纽扣怎么都扣不起来——爱玛·简会帮她的。接着,她换了双鞋,梳了梳头发。她用白色的发圈把那头卷曲的黑发扎成一根辫子。

丽贝卡冲着镜子里的自己笑了笑。她觉得自己已经准备好在第一次朗诵表演上大放光芒了。当转身离开房间的时候,她发现了自己钟爱的粉色阳伞。它跟这套粉色方格裙正好般配,而且同学们还从没见过这把阳伞。撑着它带到学校里太惹眼了,丽贝卡不会就这么把它带到教室去。她用一张纸把它包起来带走,只在表演的时候才拿出来展示一下,然后就把它带回家。

丽贝卡包扎好她的阳伞,瞟了一眼时钟。天哪!一点还差二十分,她要迟到啦!丽贝卡从边门蹦出来,在门口的玫瑰丛中摘了一朵粉色的玫瑰,然后一口气从家里跑到学校,在极短的时间内令人难以置信地跑完了一英里。她在学校门口遇见了爱玛·简,她穿得十分华丽,也是气喘吁吁的。

"丽贝卡·罗威娜·兰德尔!"爱玛·简激动地大喊,"你就像画里的一样漂亮!"

"胡说!"丽贝卡笑了起来,"是这条粉色的方格裙漂亮吧。"

"你平时可不是这么好看的,"爱玛·简坚持说,"不知

Jane. "You're different somehow today. See my garnet ring? Mother scrubbed it in soap and water so it would shine! How on earth did you convince your Aunt Miranda to let you put on your brand-new dress?"

"She and Aunt Jane weren't home when I got there, so I didn't have a chance to ask," Rebecca answered, rather anxious all of a sudden. "Why do you ask? Do you think that they would have said no?"

"Miss Miranda always says no, doesn't she?" asked Emma Jane.

"Ye-es, that's true, but this afternoon is very special — almost like a Sunday school concert, don't you think?"

"Yes, it is, with your name on the board, your flag behind us as we sing, and our elegant dialogue, and all that," Emma Jane reassured her friend.

The afternoon's performance was a succession of solid *triumphs* for everyone present. There were no failures, no tears, no parents ashamed of their offspring. Miss Dearborn's head did not ache. In fact, she heard many admiring remarks spoken about her teaching ability that afternoon.

Miss Dearborn wondered if this praise belonged to her alone, or rather partly, at least, to Rebecca. The child had had no more to do than several of her classmates, but she had remained somehow in the forefront of events. The background positively refused to hold her, yet her worst enemy could not

道为什么，你今天看起来有点不太一样。看见我的石榴子石戒指了吗？妈妈用肥皂把它擦了一遍，然后用清水冲干净，它现在看起来闪闪发亮！你究竟是怎么说服你米兰达姨妈让你穿上这件新衣服的呢？"

"我回去的时候，她和简姨妈都不在家，所以我还没来得及跟她说。"丽贝卡突然感到很紧张，"为什么这么问？难道你认为她们会说不吗？"

"米兰达小姐总是说不，难道不是吗？"爱玛·简问。

"是——的，确实是这样，不过今天下午非常特别——就像主日学校的音乐会一样，难道你不这么认为吗？"

"是的，你的大名写在黑板上，我们将在你画的国旗前面表演唱歌、文雅的对话，还有其他节目。"爱玛·简给她的朋友打气。

今天下午的演出对在场所有的人来说都是一连串的胜利。没有失败，没有泪水，没有父母为自己的孩子感到羞耻。迪尔伯恩小姐也没有头痛。事实上，那天下午，她听见许多人称赞她的能力。

迪尔伯恩小姐心想，人们的赞扬是否只属于她自己一个人，还是至少有一部分归功于丽贝卡。与班上其他几个同学相比，丽贝卡并没有做得很多；可是，不知为什么，她却处于最显著的位置。她生性活跃，可是，即便最仇恨她的人也没法把她的行为说成是咄咄逼人。她只是随时准备着并且乐

have called her pushy. She was simply ready and willing and never shy, without seeking chances for display. She remained remarkably unaware of her own talents, and instead tried to bring others into whatever fun or entertainment there was to be had. Rebecca's clear soprano voice had soared above all the rest in the choruses, and everyone had taken note of her soulful singing and endless enthusiasm. Wherever she had stood had become the focal point of the performance.

Finally, the afternoon came to an end. It seemed to Rebecca as if she would never be so cool and calm again, as she walked slowly along the path, back toward the brick house. The certainty of having to do Saturday's chores and to help make jam the next day held no terrors for her. A certain radiant joy had flooded her soul.

There were thick black clouds gathering in the sky, but Rebecca took no note of them except to be glad that the sun had been covered up so that she could put up her sunshade. She felt as if she was walking at least a foot off the ground. Rebecca continued to feel extremely happy until she entered the side yard of the brick house and saw her Aunt Miranda standing with her hands on her hips in the open doorway. Then. when she realized that her aunt was really angry with her, Rebecca came back down to earth with a rush and a thudding heart.

意站出来，从来不扭扭捏捏，但是，她也不会找机会出风头。她给其他同学带来各种乐趣和欢愉，可是，对自己的这种才能却从来没有意识。丽贝卡清晰的女高音远胜于班上合唱队里其他的学生，所有人都注意到她唱歌时全身心地投入，而且热情昂扬。她站在哪里，哪里就会成为表演的焦点。

星期五下午的会演终于结束了。丽贝卡沿着小路慢吞吞地朝砖房走去，她看上去好像再也不会冷静下来、再也不会镇定下来了。星期六的家务，还有准备第二天的果酱，这些事都没有让她感到害怕。她现在浑身充满着喜悦。

此时，天空乌云密布，不过丽贝卡并没有注意到，反而很高兴太阳躲了起来，她可以撑起那把阳伞了。她觉得自己走路好像要飘起来了。丽贝卡一路上欢天喜地，直到走进砖房的院子，看见米兰达姨妈双手插在腰间，站在敞开的大门口。当她意识到姨妈很生她的气时，丽贝卡马上又回到了地面，心怦的一下快速沉了下去。

8

INJUSTICE AT HOME

"There you are, over an hour late. A little later and you'd have been caught in a thunderstorm, but you'd never notice," Aunt Miranda *scolded* Rebecca as soon as she caught sight of her entering the house. Then she turned to Aunt Jane, and continued the display of temper that she had begun before Rebecca's arrival. "If that's not bad enough, look at her rigged out in that new dress, stepping along with her father's danc- ing-school steps, and swinging that parasol for all the world as if she were play-acting on the stage. Now I'm the oldest, Jane, and I intend to have my say once and for all. If you don't like it, you can go into the kitchen until I've finished. Step right in here, Rebecca, I want to talk to you. What did you put on that new dress for, on a school day, without permission?"

"I had intended to ask you at lunchtime, but you weren't at home, so I couldn't," began Rebecca feebly.

"You did no such thing. You put it on because you were left alone, in spite of the fact that you knew well enough that I wouldn't have let you."

八

姨妈家的不公正待遇

"你总算回来了，已经迟到了一个多小时。再晚回来一点儿，你就会遇上雷雨，可是你压根儿就没放在心上。"眼见丽贝卡走进砖房，米兰达姨妈立马开始责骂她。接着，米兰达转向简，继续发怒，其实早在丽贝卡回来之前，米兰达就已经怒不可遏了。"如果这还算不上糟糕的话，那么瞧瞧她这身新衣服，走路就像她父亲一样在跳舞，还向所有人挥动手里的阳伞，像是在舞台上演戏。简，我是家中年纪最长的人，现在我想把话一次说个清楚。如果你不爱听，可以到厨房去，直到我说完再出来。丽贝卡，到这儿来，我想跟你谈谈。你为什么不经允许就穿上新裙子去上学？"

"我原打算吃午饭的时候问你们的，可当时你们都不在家，所以我没法问。"丽贝卡有气无力地说。

"你根本没这么做。家里只有你一个人，所以你就擅自穿上它。可是，你心里清楚我不会让你穿着它去上学。"

71

"If I'd been certain you wouldn't have let me, I'd never have done it," said Rebecca, trying to be truthful. "But I wasn't certain, and it was worth risking. I thought perhaps you might let me, if you knew that it was almost a real exhibition at school."

"Exhibition!" exclaimed Miranda. "You are certainly an exhibition enough by yourself. Were you also exhibiting your parasol?" she continued sarcastically.

"The parasol was silly," confessed Rebecca, hanging her head. "But it's been the only time in my whole life that I've had anything to match it, and it looked so beautiful with the pink dress! Emma Jane and I performed a dialogue about a city girl and a country girl. It occurred to me just as I was leaving the house that the parasol would be just the right thing for the city girl to hold. It did look nice! I haven't hurt my dress at all, Aunt Miranda."

"It's the underhandedness of your actions that's the worst," said Miranda coldly. "Let's talk about the other things that you've done today. You went up the front stairs to your room, when you know that walking up those steps dirties the carpet — I found your handkerchief halfway up. You never cleared away your lunch or did the dishes. Worst of all, you left the side door unlocked from lunchtime until we got home after three o'clock. Anybody could have come in here and stolen what they liked!"

"要是我肯定您不让我穿,我是决不会穿上它的。"丽贝卡极力表现得诚实,她说,"可是,我不敢肯定,况且今天值得冒险穿上它。我想,要是您知道今天学校像是真正的展览,您可能会让我穿上它去学校。"

"展览!"米兰达大叫起来,"你确实算得上是在展览自己。你是不是还展览了你的阳伞啊?"米兰达姨妈继续挖苦她。

"这把阳伞是没有知觉的,"丽贝卡抬起头,老实地说,"不过,这是我有生以来唯一一次找到合适的东西与它搭配,而且与粉色的裙子搭配让它看上去漂亮极了!我和爱玛·简表演对话,分别扮演城里女孩和乡下女孩。当时我正要离开家,突然想到城里女孩手里该拿着阳伞,这把阳伞刚好可以用上。它确实看上去漂亮极了!米兰达姨妈,我根本没有弄坏新裙子。"

"你偷偷地做事,这是最糟糕的。"米兰达姨妈冷冷地说,"我们再来说说你今天还干了些什么事。你从前面的楼梯上去到你的卧室,那时你知道这么做会把地毯弄脏——我在楼梯上发现了你的手帕。你从来不收拾吃剩下的午饭或清洗碟子。最糟糕的是,你从边门出去的时候没有把门锁上,直到我们下午三点钟回来才发现。这样任何人都可以进来,偷走他们想要的东西!"

Rebecca sat down heavily in her chair as Aunt Miranda listed her many sins. How could she have been so careless? The tears began to flow as she attempted to explain actions that were obviously too awful to Justify or forgive.

"Oh, I'm so sony!" Rebecca wailed. "I was decorating the schoolroom, and I left late and had to run all the way home. It was hard getting into my dress alone, and I hadn't time to eat but a mouthful of bread. Just at the last minute, when I honestly — honestly — would have remembered to clear the table and wash the dishes, I looked at the clock. I knew I would have to run all the way back to school to be in time to form the line! I thought how dreadful it would be to arrive late and get my first black mark on a Friday afternoon, with the minister's wife and the doctor's wife and the school committee all there. I was in such a rush that I simply flew out the door and forgot to lock it!"

"All right, there's no need to get hysterical," Aunt Miranda said sternly. "There's no use crying over spilt milk. An ounce of good behavior would be worth a pound of sorrys and repentance, especially in your case. Take that rose out of your dress and let me look at the spot it has made on your collar and the rusty holes where the wet pin went in. It looks all right, but it's more by luck than by planning on your part. I've got no patience with your flowers and flowing locks and all your airs and graces — you put on airs just like that ne'er-do-well father of yours used to do."

当米兰达姨妈列举她的种种罪行时，丽贝卡沉重地坐到椅子上。她怎么会这么粗心大意呢？丽贝卡想要为这些恶劣的、难以饶恕的行为辩解，可是，眼泪已经忍不住夺眶而出了。

"哦，真对不起！"丽贝卡哭着说，"我在布置教室，中午回来晚了，不得不跑回家。我一个人很难把裙子扣上，我没有时间吃午饭，只吃了几口面包。我真的——真的——记得要把桌子收拾好，把碗碟洗干净，可是就在最后一刻，我看了看时钟。我知道自己不得不跑回学校，才赶得及参加演出！我心里想着，要是下午在牧师妻子、医生妻子和校董会面前迟到，那么这个星期五下午我将会得到第一个黑色标记，那该有多可怕啊！我急匆匆地从边门跑出去，才会忘了把门锁上！"

"好啦，别哭得歇斯底里的，"米兰达姨妈严厉地说，"后悔也没有用。循规蹈矩一点比得上事后一大堆道歉和忏悔，尤其像你这样的情况。把衣服上的玫瑰拿掉，让我看看你领口上的污点，还有别针留下来的锈孔。还好没弄脏，不过这只是你的运气，并不是你想要特意保护它的。我已经看够了你的玫瑰、松垂的头发，还有你的风度和优雅——你的风度就跟你那个没用的父亲一样。"

Rebecca lifted her head in a flash. Her mother had told her that she must always stand up for her father, because nothing had ever gone his way in life. He would not have died so young and so broke if he hadn't had such bad luck.

"Look here. Aunt Miranda," Rebecca said fiercely, "I'll be as good as I know how to be. I'll obey you as well as I know how. I'll never leave the door unlocked again, but I won't have my father called names. He was a p-perfectly l-lovely father. That's what he was, and it's mean to call him names."

"Don't you dare answer me back in that *impertinent* way, Rebecca! Your father was a vain, foolish, lazy man! You may as well hear it from me before you hear it from the whole town. He spent your mother's money, and he left her with seven children to provide for."

"It's s-something to leave s-seven nice children," sobbed Rebecca.

"Not when your mother has to work her lingers to the bone on that farm, just to keep the bank from taking it back. Not when other folks like your Aunt Jane and I have to help feed, clothe, and educate those seven children," Miranda said pointedly. "Now, you go upstairs and go to bed. I want you to stay in your room until morning. You'll find a bowl of crackers and milk on your dresser for dinner. I don't want to hear another sound from you until breakfast time. Jane, run

丽贝卡迅速抬起头。妈妈曾经告诉她，必须永远站在爸爸这边，因为爸爸这一生从来没有顺心过。他要是没这么倒霉，也不会穷困潦倒，年纪轻轻就去世了。

"米兰达姨妈，听我说，"丽贝卡激动地说，"我会尽量做个好孩子。我会尽量听您的话。我出门时再也不会忘了锁门，可是，我不会让人骂我爸爸。他是一个——最——好的爸爸。他就是那样的人，骂他是卑鄙的行为。"

"丽贝卡，你胆敢这么无礼地跟我顶嘴！你爸爸就是个自负、愚蠢又懒惰的家伙！不只我一个人这么说，整个镇上的人都会这么说，你听着好了。他花光了你妈妈的钱，还撇下七个孩子让她抚养。"

"是——是留下七——七个好孩子。"丽贝卡哭着说。

"你妈妈在农场上拼命地干活，就是为了保住农场不被银行没收。像我和你简姨妈这样的亲戚还得供你们这七个小孩吃的、穿的，还有上学的费用。"米兰达姨妈一针见血地指出，"现在，你上楼睡觉去。给我待在房里，明天早上以前不准下楼。晚饭时你的碗柜上会有一碗饼干和牛奶。明天吃早饭前，我不想听见你的声音。简，快去把晾在洗衣绳上

and take the dish towels off the line. We're going to have a terrible storm."

"We've had it already, I think," Jane answered quietly. "I don't often speak my mind, Miranda," she continued once she was certain that Rebecca was out of earshot, "but you ought not to have said what you did about Lorenzo Randall. He was what he was, but he was Rebecca's father. Aurelia always said that he was a good husband to her."

"Yes, but the truth needs telling, every now and then. As far as I'm concerned, that child will never amount to anything until she gets rid of what she inherited from her father, namely his imagination and his impractical, romantic notions about life.I'm glad I said just what I did."

"I dare say you are," remarked Jane, with what might be described as one of her annual bursts of courage. "But all the same, Miranda, it wasn't good manners. It wasn't very *charitable* or loving of you, either."

的洗碗布收进来。我们就要经历一场可怕的暴风雨了。"

"我想我们刚经历一场暴风雨。"简平静地说，"米兰达，我很少发表我的意见。"当她确信丽贝卡已经听不见她们说话时，接着说，"可是你不该那么指责洛伦佐·兰德尔。他就是那种人，不过他毕竟是丽贝卡的爸爸。奥里莉亚也总说他是个好丈夫。"

"是的，不过真相需要经常说出来。就我所知，除非那孩子能摆脱从她爸爸那儿继承来的坏毛病，也就是说对生活充满不切实际和罗曼蒂克的幻想，否则她将来决不会有什么出息。我很高兴我刚才说了那番话。"

"我敢说你确实如此，"简鼓起她一年难得一见的勇气，说，"可是，米兰达，这不是什么有教养的行为，而且也显得你很不宽厚、仁爱。"

9

THE WOULD-BE RUNAWAY

Rebecca closed the door to her room wearily. She took off the beloved pink gingham dress with trembling fingers. She smoothed it out carefully, *pinched* up the white ruffle at the front, and laid it away in her drawer with a little sob at the idea of the roughness of life. The withered pink rose she had been holding fell to the floor. Rebecca thought to herself, "Just like my happy day!"

Nothing showed quite so clearly the intelligent child she was than the fact that she instantly recognized the symbolism of the rose. She laid it in the drawer with her dress, as if she were burying the whole episode with all of its sad memories. It was a child's poetic instinct with a *dawning hint* of womanly feeling in it.

Rebecca combed her hair. All the while, the resolve grew in her mind that she would leave the brick house and go back to her beloved Sunnybrook Farm. She would not be taken back with open arms — there were too many children for that —

九

差点离家出走

丽贝卡疲惫地关上房门。她用颤抖的手指脱下心爱的粉色方格裙。她小心翼翼地把裙子将平，揉揉前面裙摆上的白花边，然后把它放进抽屉。一想到生活的艰辛，她就忍不住轻声哭泣。原先她一直拿在手里的玫瑰枯萎了，掉落到地上。丽贝卡心想："它就像这快乐的一天！"

她马上就意识到玫瑰的象征意义，没什么比这更能说明她是个聪明的孩子。她把玫瑰跟衣服一起放进抽屉，仿佛在埋葬一段痛苦的回忆。这是孩子充满诗意的本能，略带些女性的多愁善感。

丽贝卡梳了梳头。突然，脑子里冒出一个念头。她决定离开这座砖房，回到她深爱的太阳溪农场。家里人不会张开双臂欢迎她——因为家里的孩子实在太多了——可是，她能

but she would help her mother with the house and send Hannah to Riverboro in her place. "I hope she'll like it better than I have," Rebecca thought in a momentary burst of temper.

Rebecca sat down by the window and watched the rain streaming down. She had hoped that Aunt Miranda would be pleased that her niece had succeeded so well at school, but there seemed no hope of pleasing her — in that respect or in any other. Rebecca would just have to go back to Maplewood on the stage the next day with Mr. Cobb, and then get cousin Ann to take her back to the farm. She would slip away without telling her aunts that she was leaving. They would find her gone before breakfast.

Rebecca never stopped very long to think through a plan. Once she had decided to run away, she put on her oldest clothes and shoes. Then she wrapped her nightgown, comb, and toothbrush in a pillowcase, and dropped the small bundle softly out of her bedroom window. She scrambled out of the window after it, then flew up the road in the rainstorm.

Jeremiah Cobb was sitting at his kitchen table when he caught sight of Rebecca at his back door. Rebecca's face was so swollen with tears and so full of misery that for a moment he scarcely recognized her. His big heart went out to her in her trouble. He wanted her to be the first to tell him of it, so he decided that he would pretend that he hadn't noticed anything was wrong.

帮助妈妈干活，让汉纳到利佛保罗顶替她。"希望她会比我更喜欢这个地方。"丽贝卡顿时觉得心里有气。

丽贝卡坐在窗边，看着外面的瓢泼大雨。她原来希望米兰达姨妈会对侄女在学校里取得的成绩感到满意，可是现在看来没法讨好她——不管用什么样的方法。丽贝卡只能明天搭乘科布先生的公共马车去枫林，然后让安表姐送她回农场。她打算偷偷地溜走，不告诉两位姨妈。等到第二天吃早饭的时候她们才会察觉她逃走了。

丽贝卡从来不会花太多时间去思考某个计划。一旦打定主意，她立刻换上来时的旧衣服和旧鞋子。她把睡衣、梳子和牙刷裹到枕头套里，把它从卧室窗口轻轻地扔了下去。然后，她沿着窗户往下爬，冒着暴风雨飞奔到大路上。

杰里迈亚·科布坐在自家厨房的桌旁，这时，看见丽贝卡出现在他家后门口。丽贝卡的脸因为泪水和痛苦肿了起来，以至于杰里迈亚一时间没有认出她。他心里清楚，丽贝卡遇到了麻烦。他想让她第一个告诉自己，所以他决定假装没有察觉不对劲的地方。

"Well, I never! It's my little lady passenger! Come to call on us, have you? You come right in and dry yourself by the stove. Mrs. Cobb has gone to nurse old Seth Strout through a bad case of the flu, but you'll stay and have a cup of tea with me, won't you?" he coaxed.

"Oh, Mr. Cobb, I've run away from the brick house, and I want to go back to the farm!" Rebecca cried. "Will you and Mrs. Cobb let me stay here tonight and take me up to Maplewood in the stage in the morning? I haven't got any money for my fare, but I'll earn it somehow afterwards and I'll send it to you."

"Well, we certainly won't argue over money, you and I. But I'd like to hear why you've decided to leave us before we've even had the opportunity to go to the fair together at Milltown. Why don't you tell me what has happened?"

Rebecca recounted the history of her trouble. Tragic as that history seemed to her passionate mind, she told it truthfully and without exaggeration. Mr. Cobb did not interrupt. He listened carefully to her tale, and tried to think of a way to resolve this terrible situation for the good of all concerned.

"哦，真不敢相信！原来是我的小乘客！你是来看望我们的，是吗？快进来，到炉子旁把衣服烤烤干。老塞思·斯特劳特得了严重的流感，科布太太去照料他了。不过，你可以留下来跟我一起喝杯咖啡，怎么样？"杰里迈亚耐心地说。

"哦，科布先生，我刚从砖房逃出来，我想回农场去！"丽贝卡哭了起来，"你和科布太太能不能让我在这过一夜，明天一早带我坐马车去枫林？我现在没钱付车费，不过以后我会把赚来的钱寄给您的。"

"哦，我们当然不会为了钱而吵起来。但是，我想知道为什么你决定离开我们，要知道，我们还没机会一起去看米尔顿城的集市呢。为什么不告诉我到底发生了什么事呢？"

丽贝卡把她遇到的麻烦一股脑儿讲给杰里迈亚听。她老老实实地讲述，一点儿都不夸张。这番遭遇对感情强烈的丽贝卡来说显得过于悲惨。科布先生没有打断她。他仔细地听她讲述，并且设法找到一个两全其美的办法来解决眼前这桩棘手的事儿。

10

A TRICKY RETURN

"You will take me to Maplewood, won't you, Mr. Cobb?" Rebecca pleaded as she ended her narrative.

"Don't you fret," he answered, planning his replies carefully. "I'll see the lady passenger through her trouble somehow. Now, sit down and have a bite of something to eat. Spread some of that good jam Mrs. Cobb makes on that piece of bread. Would you be so kind as to pour me another cup of tea?"

Comforted by the old man's tone, Rebecca began to enjoy the *dignity* of sitting in Mrs. Cobb's seat. She smoothed her hair, dried her eyes, and poured tea for both of them from the blue china teapot.

"I suppose your mother will be awfully glad to see you back home again," Mr. Cobb began.

"She won't like it that I ran away, and she'll be sorry that I couldn't succeed at pleasing Aunt Miranda. But I'll make her understand," Rebecca explained.

十
巧妙的劝回

"科布先生，你会带我去枫林的，不是吗？"丽贝卡讲完自己的遭遇后恳求他。

"别着急，"他慎重地回答，"不管怎么样，我都会帮助我的女乘客渡过难关。现在，坐下来，吃点东西。在面包上涂点科布太太做的好吃的果酱。你能再帮我倒杯茶吗？"

丽贝卡从老人的话语中得到了安慰，于是，她坐在科布太太的位子上，享受这份礼遇。她梳理了一下头发，擦干眼泪，拿起蓝瓷茶壶给自己和科布先生各斟了一杯茶。

"我想，你妈妈见到你回去肯定非常高兴。"科布先生开始说话。

"她不喜欢我逃跑出来，而且她会为我没能讨米兰达姨妈欢心而感到难过。可是，我会让她谅解的。"丽贝卡解释说。

"I suppose she was thinking of your education by sending you here in the first place." Mr. Cobb pointed out. "But you can go to school back in Temperance."

"They have school only two months of the year in Temperance, but the farm's too far away from all the other schools," Rebecca replied. She was a little less sure of her plans all of a sudden.

"Oh, well, there are other things in this world besides education," Mr. Cobb continued, attacking a piece of apple pie.

"Ye-es, though Mother thought that education would be the making of me," Rebecca said sadly, choking back a *sob* as she tried to drink her tea.

"It will be nice for you to be all together again on the farm — such a house full of children!"

"It's too full — that's the trouble. I'll make my sister Hannah come to Riverboro in my place."

"What if Miranda and Jane don't want any more of you to come? Your aunts will be kind of mad at you for running away, you know. You can't really blame them for being upset about that," Mr. Cobb argued.

This was quite a new thought — that the brick house might be closed to Hannah, once her sister Rebecca had turned her back upon its cold hospitality.

"No use talking about it, anymore." Mr. Cobb shrugged, then pursued another strategy. "How's the school down here in Riverboro — pretty good?"

"我想她当初把你送到这儿来是为你的学业着想,"科布先生指出,"不过,你可以回汤普朗斯上学。"

"汤普朗斯的学校每年只上两个月的课,而其他学校离农场又很远。"丽贝卡回答。她突然对自己的计划稍稍有些动摇。

"哦,好吧,除了上学,这世上还有别的事情可以做。"科布先生咬了一片苹果派,接着说。

"是——的,可是,妈妈认为上学能让我变得有出息。"丽贝卡伤心地说。她忍住不哭,想要喝口茶。

"对你来说回到农场与家人团聚是件好事——那有一屋子的小孩!"

"屋里挤满了人——那很麻烦。我会让我的姐姐汉纳来利佛保罗顶替我。"

"要是米兰达和简并不想你们家其他孩子过来该怎么办?你知道,你的出走会把两位姨妈气疯的。你真的不能怪她们这么做。"科布先生辩解说。

这完全是丽贝卡没有想到的——砖房的大门可能会对汉纳关闭,谁让丽贝卡冷冷地拒绝了姨妈的好意呢。

"没必要再谈论这个问题了。"科布先生耸耸肩,又想到了另一个计策。"利佛保罗的学校怎么样,很不错吧?"

"Oh, it's a splendid school! Miss Dearborn is a wonderful teacher!" Rebecca exclaimed excitedly.

"You like her, do you? Well, she certainly returns your feelings. Mrs. Cobb was down at the store this afternoon. She met Miss Dearborn on the bridge on her way back home. They got to talking about school. 'How is the little girl from Temperance doing?' my wife asks. 'Oh, she's the best scholar I have!' says Miss Dearborn. 'I could teach school from sunrise to sunset if all my scholars were as bright and as willing as Rebecca Randall.'"

"She said that?" glowed Rebecca, her smile dimpling in an instant. "I'll study the covers right off the books after this!"

"You mean, you would study that hard if you had decided to stay here in Riverboro," Mr. Cobb reminded her. "But you've decided to give it up because you're so angry with that Miranda Sawyer. Not that I blame you for being mad. She's cranky and she's sour, like she's been eating green apples all her life. She is difficult, and you're not a very patient person, I guess."

"No, I guess I'm not a very patient person," Rebecca admitted.

"Well, you're not wrong to lose patience with your aunt. She's terribly hard to please. Plus, she kind of heaves benefits at your head as if they were bricks. Although, she does give you new clothes, and a good place to live, and a fine education. Those are all benefits that you may eventually help repay with your good behavior.

"哦，这所学校太棒了！迪尔伯恩小姐也是个很好的老师！"丽贝卡激动地嚷嚷。

"你喜欢她，是吗？其实她对你也不错啊。科布太太今天下午去店里买东西。回来时在桥上碰到迪尔伯恩小姐。她们谈起了学校的事情。'从汤普朗斯来的那个小姑娘在学校表现怎么样？'我妻子问。'哦，她是我最好的学生！'迪尔伯恩小姐说，'要是所有的学生都像丽贝卡·兰德尔那么聪明、好学，那我可以从早教到晚。'"

"她是那么说的吗？"丽贝卡容光焕发，马上笑开了颜。"以后我要努力学习，把书本都翻烂！"

"你是说，如果你决定留在利佛保罗，就会努力学习。"科布先生提醒她，"可是，你因为生米兰达·索耶的气就决定放弃了。我倒不是怪你生气。她这人既古怪又爱发脾气，就像她这辈子都在吃青苹果。她很难相处，我想你也不是个有耐心的人吧。"

"是的，我想我并不是个有耐心的人。"丽贝卡承认。

"好吧，对姨妈不耐烦并不是你的错。想讨好她是非常困难的。另外，她还喜欢把对你的恩惠挂在嘴边，让你觉得受到了侮辱。可是，她给你新衣服穿，供你地方住，还让你接受良好的教育。她为你做了那么多事，你该好好表现来报答她。"

"Is your Aunt Jane any easier to get along with?" Mr. Cobb asked, changing his tactics yet again.

"Oh, Aunt Jane and I get along splendidly," said Rebecca. "She's just as good and as kind as she can be. I like her better all the time. I'd let her scold me all day long, for I feel that she understands me."

"Your Aunt Jane will probably be very sorry tomorrow morning when she finds out that you've gone away. But, never mind, it can't be helped. She no doubt enjoys your company a great deal. In fact, Mrs. Cobb told me the other day that she had seen your Aunt Jane in town. 'You wouldn't know the brick house,' Jane said to her. 'I'm keeping a sewing school, and my student has sewn three beautiful dresses, the latest in pink gingham. I'm even thinking of reliving my youth by going to the church picnic with Rebecca!' According to my wife, it seemed pretty clear that Jane Sawyer had never looked so young or so happy."

Mr. Cobb knew that those final words had hit home. There was a silence that could be felt in the little kitchen, a silence made louder by the fact that the rain had stopped outside. A rainbow had appeared, visible from the kitchen window in the early evening light. Mr. Cobb seemed to have built another rainbow over Rebecca's troubles, one that would lead her happily back to the brick house.

"The storm's over," Mr. Cobb said with a wink and a smile.

"你那位简姨妈是不是比较容易相处啊?"科布先生问。他再次改变策略。

"哦,我跟简姨妈处得好极了,"丽贝卡说,"她正是那种温柔、善良的人。我一直都是比较喜欢她。我宁愿她整天责备我,因为我觉得她能理解我。"

"明天早上,你简姨妈发现你逃走后可能会很难过。可是,别介意,那没什么用。毫无疑问,有你做伴她获得了许多快乐。其实,科布太太前几天告诉我,她在镇上见到你简姨妈。'你不知道,在砖房里,'简对她说,'我开了一所缝纫学校,我的学生缝了三件漂亮的衣服,最后一件是粉色的方格裙。我甚至考虑跟丽贝卡一起去教堂野餐,重新找回我的青春!'根据我妻子的描述,很显然,简·索耶看上去从来没有这么年轻、这么快乐过。"

科布先生知道最后几句话击中了要害。此时,厨房里一片寂静。外面的暴风雨停了,这使得他家的小厨房显得更加安静。傍晚时分,天边出现了一道彩虹,从厨房窗口望出去可以看见。科布先生好似为丽贝卡筑起了另一道跨过烦恼的彩虹,它指引着丽贝卡快乐地回到砖房。

"暴风雨过去了,"科布先生眨眨眼,笑着说,"这场雨

"It has cleared the air and washed the face of the earth nice and clean. Tomorrow, everything will shine like a new pin."

"Yes, tomorrow will mean a new day and a fresh start. I'm going to stay here and — and catch some bricks if I have to. I'm going to catch them without throwing them back, either," Rebecca said, grinning.

Mr. Cobb drove her back home and helped her sneak back through the window of her bedroom. Her aunts were never made aware that she had planned to run away. When Rebecca found herself back in her own bed that night, she felt a kind of peace stealing over her. She had been saved from foolishness and error. She had been kept from troubling her poor mother and embarrassing her aunts. Her heart was melted now. She felt determined to win her Aunt Miranda's approval.

It would have been some comfort to Rebecca if she had known that Miranda Sawyer had passed an equally uncomfortable night. She regretted her words and her harshness to the point where she made a promise to try to be less severe with her niece in the future.

让空气变得清新，让大地变得干净、美好。明天，一切都会像崭新的胸针那样闪闪发亮。"

"是的，明天意味着新的一天和新的开始。我会留在这里——万不得已我也会挨姨妈的训。我不再跟她顶嘴。"丽贝卡哧哧地笑着说。

科布先生赶车送丽贝卡回到砖房，帮助她偷偷地从窗口爬进卧室。两位姨妈从没察觉她曾想要离家出走。那天晚上，丽贝卡躺在自己的床上，感到一阵安宁向她袭来。她从愚蠢和错误的边缘被挽救回来。她没有给可怜的妈妈带来麻烦，也没有让两位姨妈感到丢脸。她现在释怀了。她决定赢得米兰达姨妈对她的认可。

假如丽贝卡知道米兰达·索耶那天晚上也不好过，那她多少会觉得安慰些。米兰达后悔自己对丽贝卡说了那番话，对她过于严厉，她发誓今后对侄女不再那么严厉。

11

THE BANQUET LAMP

Just before the *Thanksgiving* of Rebecca's fourteenth year, the affairs of her friends, the Simpsons, reached what might have been called a crisis, even in their family. The Simpsons had long suffered from poverty and uncertainty. Mr. Simpson had spent his whole life taking things from neighbors without asking and with no intention of returning them. He considered what he did "borrowing" — taking items that were not in active use from his neighbors' barns and fields.

Mr. Simpson's neighbors didn't see his behavior in the same way that he did, however. They called it stealing. Mr. Simpson had been caught and sent to jail recently for stealing, and this left his family even worse off than ever. There was little to eat and less to wear, although Mrs. Simpson did, as always, her very best to provide for her children.

In the chill of a *gloomy* early September, with the vision of other people's plump turkeys, corn, squash, and pumpkins being gathered into barns, the young Simpsons looked for some

十一

宴会灯

　　就在丽贝卡即将迎来第十四个感恩节前夕,她的朋友辛普森家的孩子,甚至可以说是他们一家遇到了我们常说的危机。辛普森一家长期以来生活贫困,没有固定的收入。辛普森先生向来都是一声不吭地拿走邻居的东西,而且也不打算归还。他自认为这种行为是"借"——从邻居家的谷仓和田地里拿走他们不经常用的东西。

　　然而,辛普森的邻居可不这么认为。他们把辛普森的所作所为叫做偷窃。最近,辛普森先生被抓起来,关进了监狱,这使得他的家人生活比以前更加窘迫。尽管辛普森太太一如既往尽力地照顾孩子,可他们家还是吃不饱、穿不暖。

　　在寒冷、阴沉的九月初,眼看别人忙着把肥嘟嘟的火鸡、玉米,还有西葫芦和南瓜搬进谷仓,辛普森家的孩子想法寻求某些廉价的刺激。他们决定通过卖肥皂来赢得奖品。

inexpensive form of excitement. They settled upon the idea of selling soap for prizes. They sold enough to their neighbors during the months of September and October to win a children's wagon. This wagon was not well made, but they had fun giving one another rides over bumpy country roads.

In November, the Simpson children set their sights on a more *ambitious* prize: a banquet lamp, which looked to be about eight feet tall in the catalogue of prizes issued by the soap company. It was made of polished brass, but often mistaken for solid gold, according to the description in the catalogue. The shade that accompanied it as a prize for selling an extra hundred bars of soap was of crinkled crepe paper in "a dozen top-choice decorator colors".

Seesaw Simpson, a boy of fourteen who scoffed at the idea of selling soap, was not part of the sales team. Clara Belle Simpson was a fairly successful door-to-door salesperson, but Susan, who lisped and could only say "thoap", never sold a bar. The twins, who were too young to be trusted thoroughly, were given only six bars at a time. They were sent on their rounds with a document stating the price per bar, per dozen, and per box of one hundred bars.

Rebecca and her friend Emma Jane offered to help on a day when they were going to travel three or four miles by wagon to see Emma Jane's cousins in North Riverboro. They wanted to see what they could do in the way of stirring up popular

在九月和十月这两个月里，他们向邻居兜售肥皂，换来了一辆儿童货车。这辆车子做工并不好，可是他们仍然很高兴赶着车在乡间崎岖不平的路上来回奔波。

到了十一月，辛普森家的孩子雄心勃勃，把眼光投向更大的奖品——一盏宴会灯。从肥皂公司发放的奖品目录上看，这盏灯大概有八英尺高。根据目录上的介绍，它是用黄铜制成，经过抛光，不过人们常常误以为它是纯金的。再多卖掉一百条肥皂，就可以得到用绉纱做的灯罩，这种灯罩有"十二种最好的装饰性的颜色可供选择"。

西索·辛普森这个十四岁大的男孩，他嘲笑卖肥皂的计划，并没有参与到推销的队伍中。克拉拉·贝尔·辛普森是个相当成功的上门推销员，可是，苏珊口齿不清，把"肥皂"发成"浮皂"，结果一条肥皂都没卖出去。双胞胎年纪还小，办事不太牢靠，所以每次只给他们六条肥皂。而且给他们分别写明每条肥皂的单价，以及每打肥皂、每盒肥皂（共有一百条）的价格。

丽贝卡和她的朋友爱玛·简主动提出帮助他们推销一天，那天她们要去北利佛保罗看望爱玛·简的表兄妹。她们

demand for the Snow-White and Rose-Red brand — the former a laundry soap and the latter intended for use in the bath.

Rebecca and Emma Jane had a lot of fun preparing their sales pitch in Emma Jane's attic. They had the soap company's standard speech to memorize. They also remembered the dramatic delivery of a similar speech given by a patent-medicine salesman when he was working at the Milltown Fair. His method of persuasion, once observed, could never be forgotten. Rebecca practiced it on Emma Jane, and then they reversed roles.

"Can I sell you a little soap this afternoon? It is called the Snow-White and Rose-Red brand, twelve bars in a decorative box, only twenty cents for the white and twenty-five for the red. This soap is made from the purest ingredients. The ingredients are so pure that they could indeed be eaten by any invalid without doing the slightest harm," Rebecca began.

"Oh, Rebecca, let's not say that!" Emma Jane interrupted, laughing. "It makes me feel like a fool."

"It doesn't take a lot to make you feel like a fool, Emma Jane Perkins. I don't feel like a fool quite so easily. All right, leave out the eating part if you don't like it. But don't blame me if you can't sell as much soap as I do. Now you go on," Rebecca insisted.

"The Snow-White brand is probably the most remarkable laundry soap ever manufactured," Emma Jane continued. "Soak

想看看能否刺激顾客对"雪白"和"玫红"牌肥皂的大量需求——前者用来洗衣，后者用来洗澡。

在爱玛·简的阁楼上，丽贝卡和她准备了许多有趣的推销词。她们记得肥皂公司那番绝妙的推销词。她们还记得，那个在米尔顿城集市上推销药品的推销员，他当时的推销词跟这类似，引起了很大的反响。一旦见识过他的游说口才，就会让人终身难忘。首先由丽贝卡扮演推销员，向爱玛·简推销肥皂；然后，两人互换角色。

"今天下午您要买肥皂吗？这个牌子叫'雪白'和'玫红'。包装盒里有十二条肥皂，白色的只需要二十美分，红色的也只要二十五美分。这种肥皂是用最纯粹的原料制成。即便病人吃了它，也不会有一点点伤害。"丽贝卡开始推销。

"哦，丽贝卡，别这么说！"爱玛·简笑着打断她，"这让我觉得像个傻瓜。"

"这听起来一点都不像傻瓜，爱玛·简·珀金。我可不觉得这像傻瓜。好吧，要是你不喜欢，那就把吃的那段删掉。不过，到时候你卖得比我少可别怪我啊。现在，轮到你了。"丽贝卡坚持说。

"'雪白'牌肥皂很可能是目前生产的最神奇的洗衣肥皂，"爱玛·简接着推销，"把你的衣服浸泡在水里，然后把

your clothes in water, rubbing all spots lightly with the soap. Leave them overnight, and in the morning the youngest baby could wash them clean without the slightest effort."

"Babe, not baby," corrected Rebecca, looking at the brochure.

"It's the exact same thing," argued Emma Jane.

"Of course it's the same thing, but a baby has got to be called a babe or infant in our sales pitch. It has to sound the same way it would in poetry. Would you rather use the word infant?"

"No," grumbled Emma Jane, "infant is even worse than babe. Rebecca, don't you think it would be a good idea to experiment with what it claims in this part about babes washing laundry? We could have Elijah and Elisha try out the soap before we begin advertising it in this way."

"I can't imagine a baby doing the laundry with any brand of soap," answered Rebecca. "It must be possible, or they would never dare print such a thing. Let's just take the soap company's claims on faith. Oh, won't we have fun, Emma Jane? At some of the houses where they don't know me at all, I won't be a bit nervous. I shall give the whole speech — invalid, babe, and all! Perhaps I shall even say the last sentence, if I can remember it: "We sound every chord in the great macrocosm of satisfaction.' Isn't that grand?"

肥皂涂在肮脏的地方，轻轻地搓洗。浸泡一夜后第二天早上，就连家里最小的孩子也能不费吹灰之力把衣服洗得干干净净。"

"是小孩，不是孩子。"丽贝卡看着宣传册，纠正她的发音。

"这是一回事。"爱玛·简争辩说。

"当然是一回事，不过，在我们的推销词中，孩子这个词应该说成小孩或者幼儿。就像在诗歌中一样。你愿意用幼儿这个词吗？"

"不，"爱玛·简抱怨，"幼儿比小孩更差劲。丽贝卡，难道你不认为把宣传册上提到的让小孩洗衣服这段付诸实践是好主意吗？我们可以在推销前让伊莱贾和伊莱沙试用这种肥皂。"

"不管用什么牌子的肥皂，我都没法想象让一个小孩来洗衣服。"丽贝卡回答说，"不过这极有可能是真的，否则他们不敢把这些话印出来。还是让我们相信肥皂公司的广告词吧。哦，爱玛·简，这不是很有意思吗？在一些不认识我的人面前，我一点儿都不会感到紧张。我的推销词一套接着一套——什么病人啦、小孩啦，统统说出来！要是我还记得最后一句话怎么说来着，我会说：'我们将竭尽所能满足顾客的需求。'那不是很棒吗？"

12

SNOW-WHITE AND ROSE-RED

Cmma Jane and Rebecca prepared and practiced their soap-selling speech all of Friday afternoon and evening. Saturday was the big sales event. The pair would have the old white horse, so that they could drive themselves to North Riverboro, eat lunch with Emma Jane's cousins, and return at four o'clock on the dot.

When the girls asked Mrs. Perkins if they could stop at just a few houses on their way to and from North Riverboro to sell a few bars of soap, Mrs. Perkins was not so sure that this was a good idea. She did not mind her daughter amusing herself in this way, but she was nervous about letting the niece of the difficult Miranda Sawyer do such a thing. However, the girls persuaded her that they were doing it to help the Simpsons get a banquet lamp by Christmas, and Mrs. Perkins finally agreed.

The girls stopped by Mr. Watson's dry-goods store, and arranged for three hundred-bar boxes of soap to be charged

十二

"雪白"和"玫红"

　　整个星期五下午和晚上，丽贝卡和爱玛·简都在准备、练习她们的肥皂推销词。星期六是推销的大日子。两个女孩子套上一匹老白马，这样她们就可以自己赶车去北利佛保罗，然后在爱玛·简的表兄妹家吃午饭，下午四点准时回来。

　　两个女孩问珀金太太，她们可不可以在往返北利佛保罗的路上停下来，卖一些肥皂给当地人。珀金太太不敢肯定这是个好主意。她倒并不介意自己的女儿这么取乐，只是担心让难缠的米兰达·索耶她的侄女参与这件事会惹来麻烦。然而，女孩子们说，这么做是为了帮助辛普森家的孩子在圣诞节时能得到一盏宴会灯，这个理由说服了辛普森太太，最后她终于同意了。

　　女孩子们在沃森的店门前停下来，根据克拉拉·贝尔·辛普森的账目提取了装有三百条肥皂的几个大箱子。这些货

to Clara Belle Simpson's account. These were lifted onto the back of the wagon. A happier pair never drove out along the country road leading to North Riverboro. It was a *glorious* Indian summer day. There were still many leaves on the oaks and maples, making a good show of autumn color for early November. The air was like *sparkling cider*. Every field had heaps of squash and potatoes ready for the barn and the market. Rebecca stood up in the wagon and recited a poem that she had composed for the glory of the day:

> *"Great, wide, beautiful, wonderful World,*
> *With the wonderful water 'round you curled,*
> *The wonderful grass upon your breast, World, you are*
> *beautifully dressed!"*

The beauty of the day was not necessarily enough for success at selling soap, however. After an hour's worth of taking turns holding the horse and approaching potential customers, Emma Jane had only managed to sell three individual bars. Rebecca had sold three small boxes of a dozen bars each. Housewives looked at Emma Jane and desired no soap. They listened to her description of its merits and advantages, and still desired none. Rebecca's innate spark and gift of speech made her a more effective salesperson. The people with whom she conversed either remembered their current need of soap, or reminded themselves that they would need some at some point in the future. But neither girl had sold enough, and both were growing rather tired and disheartened in the face of rejection.

物被搬上货车后面。这两个快乐的小姑娘从来没有在去北利佛保罗的乡间小路上亲自驾车。这天秋高气爽。橡树和枫树上还挂着许多叶子，显示了十一月初秋的色彩。空气里弥漫着苹果酒的味道。每块田里都堆起了南瓜和马铃薯，准备放进谷仓，然后拿到市场上去卖。丽贝卡站在货车上，开始朗诵她为这美好的一天所作的诗歌：

> "伟大的、宽广的、美丽的、神奇的世界，
>   奇妙的河流绕着你蜿蜒而行，
>   葱翠的青草在你的胸脯蔓延，
>   世界啊，你装扮得多么美丽！"

然而，美好的一天不见得对兜售肥皂有多大帮助。两个女孩子轮流驾车；一个小时后她们接近有需求的顾客群了。爱玛·简只卖掉三条肥皂。而丽贝卡卖了三盒肥皂，每盒有十二条。家庭主妇看见爱玛·简就没有想买肥皂的冲动。听她介绍完肥皂的优点和功用后，还是不想买。丽贝卡天生的演说才能使她成为一名更有说服力的推销员。跟她交谈过的顾客，要么想起现在家里正好缺肥皂，要么想买一些备着以后用。但是，两个女孩子卖得都太少，面对人们拒绝的表情，她们开始感到疲倦和失望。

107

"It's your turn, Rebecca, and I'm glad, too," said Emma Jane wearily. "I'm not sure who lives here. It doesn't look like anyone is at home right now. If no one answers, you'll have to take the next house, too. It will still be your turn — I'm really tired!"

Rebecca went up the driveway to the side door of a big farmhouse, where there was a large porch. Seated in a rocking chair was a good-looking man. Rebecca couldn't tell if he was young or middle-aged. He had an air of the city about him. He had a well-shaven face, well-trimmed mustache, and nicely tailored clothes. Rebecca found herself a little shy at the idea of asking such a man if he needed soap. But it was too late to do anything else except explain what she was doing standing in the middle of his driveway.

"Excuse me, sir," she began. "Is the lady of the house at home?"

"I am the lady of the house, at the present moment," said the stranger with an amused smile. "What can I do for you?"

"Have you ever heard of the — would you like, I mean — do you need any soap?" Rebecca asked haltingly.

"Do I look as if I need soap?" he joked.

Rebecca smiled, her dimples flashing. "I didn't mean that. I have some soap to sell. I mean, I would like to introduce to you a very remarkable soap, the best now on the market. It's called the — "

"丽贝卡，真高兴这次轮到你啦。"爱玛·简疲倦地说，"我不知道这里住的是谁。看上去好像现在家里没人。如果你敲门没人应答，那么你得接着去下一户人家。还是应该轮到你——我实在太累了。"

丽贝卡沿着车道走到一座气派的农舍的边门，那里有一个大门廊。一个漂亮的男人坐在摇椅里。丽贝卡说不上来他是年轻人还是中年人。他身上透着一股城里人的气度。他的脸很整洁，胡子也修得很漂亮，衣服的做工相当考究。丽贝卡发现自己一想到要向这个人推销肥皂就觉得有点害羞。不过现在打退堂鼓已经太迟了，她只能解释自己为什么会出现在他家的车道上。

"对不起，先生，"她说，"请问这家的女主人在吗？"

"现在，我就是这个家的女主人，"陌生人带着愉快的笑容说，"有什么地方能为你效劳吗？"

"你有没有听过——你喜欢，我的意思是——你需要肥皂吗？"丽贝卡吞吞吐吐地说。

"我看上去像是需要肥皂吗？"他说了句玩笑话。

丽贝卡笑了，脸上的酒窝泛起了红晕。"我不是那个意思。我有些肥皂要卖。我的意思是，我想向您介绍现在市面上最有效、最好用的肥皂。它叫——"

Rebecca continued, suddenly remembering her sales pitch in full.

"Oh! Wait a minute!" the gentleman interrupted. "I think I know the soap to which you refer. Made out of the purest vegetable fat, isn't it?"

"The very purest," echoed Rebecca.

"And a child could do the Monday washing with it and use no force to scrub out the dirt."

"A babe," corrected Rebecca.

"Oh! A babe, is it, now? That child grows younger every year!"

This was good luck, indeed, to find a customer who knew all the qualities and merits of this particular brand of soap. Rebecca accepted an invitation to sit down on a stool near the edge of the porch. She pointed out all the decorative features of the box that held a dozen bars of the Rose-Red soap. She gave her prices per bar, per box, and per case of both the Rose-Red and the Snow-White varieties. The conversation soon went from soap to other topics. Soon Rebecca forgot all about Emma Jane waiting at the gate. She chattered away as if she had known this grand gentleman in the rocking chair all her life.

丽贝卡说着说着，一下子全想起了她的推销词。

"哦，等一下！"这位绅士打断她的话，"我想我知道你所说的这种肥皂。它是用最纯粹的植物油提炼而成的，对吧？"

"是最最纯粹的。"丽贝卡重复了一遍。

"而且孩子可以在星期一用它来洗衣服，毫不费力就能搓掉污渍。"

"是小孩。"丽贝卡纠正他。

"哦，现在变成小孩啦？这孩子一年比一年小啊！"

真幸运，能够碰到这么一个顾客，他对这个牌子的肥皂的优点和功用了解得那么清楚。丽贝卡接受他的邀请，坐到门廊边的凳子上。她给绅士指出装有一打"玫红"牌肥皂的包装盒上所有的装饰特点。然后，告诉他每条肥皂、每盒肥皂，甚至每箱"玫红"和"雪白"牌肥皂的价格。他们的谈话很快从肥皂转移到其他话题上。不一会儿，丽贝卡完全忘了爱玛·简还在大门口等她。她滔滔不绝地说话，好像早就认识这个坐在摇椅里的男人。

13

THE SOAP SALE OF THE CENTURY

"I'm keeping house today, but I don't live here," explained the delightful gentleman, as he and Rebecca continued their conversation on the porch. "I'm just on an extended vacation with my aunt, who has gone to Portland to visit some relatives. I used to live in this region as a boy. I am very fond of this part of the world."

"I don't think anything takes the place of the farm where one lived when one was a child," observed Rebecca in her fanciest English.

"So, you consider your childhood a thing of the past, do you, young lady?"

"I can still remember it," answered Rebecca seriously, "though it seems a long time ago."

"I can certainly remember mine. A particularly unpleasant one it was, too!" said the stranger.

十三

肥皂大卖

"我今天在管家，可是我并不住在这里。"这个快活的绅士解释说，丽贝卡和他在门廊上继续聊天。"我刚巧到姨妈家度假，她去波特兰^①探望几个亲戚。我小时候曾经在这里住过。我非常喜欢这片土地。"

"我认为，没有什么能够取代一个人小时候住过的农场。"丽贝卡用她奇特的英语说。

"那么，你认为自己的童年已经是过去时了，是吗，小姐？"

"尽管它已是很久以前的事了，"丽贝卡严肃地说，"可是，我还记得我的童年。"

"我的确记得自己的童年。那也是一段特别让人不愉快的往事！"陌生人说。

——————————
① 美国俄勒冈北部城市

113

"So was mine," sighed Rebecca. "What was your worst trouble?"

"Lack of food and clothes, for the most part," he answered.

"Oh!" exclaimed Rebecca in *sympathy*. "Mine was no shoes and too many brothers and sisters and not enough books. But you're all right and much happier now, aren't you?" she asked. He looked handsome and well-fed and wealthy. Yet anyone who looked closely could see that his eyes were tired and his mouth droped sadly whenever he was not speaking.

"I'm doing pretty well, now. Thank you very much for inquiring," said the man with a broad smile. "Now, tell me, how much soap do you think I should buy from you today?"

"How much does your aunt have in storage now?" suggested the experienced sales agent. "And how much does she generally use?"

"Oh, I haven't the slightest idea, but soap keeps for a long time, doesn't it?"

"I'm not certain, but I have the brochure right here in my pocket. I can look it up for you," Rebecca answered truthfully, as she drew the document from her dress pocket.

"What are you going to do with the magnificent profits you get from this business?" Rebecca's customer asked.

"We are not selling for our own benefit," Rebecca confided. "My friend Emma Jane, who is holding the horse at the gate, is the daughter of a very rich blacksmith. She doesn't need

"我也是。"丽贝卡叹了口气，问，"你当时最大的烦恼是什么？"

"最主要的就是吃不饱、穿不暖。"他回答。

"哦！"丽贝卡同情地说，"我最大的烦恼就是没有鞋子穿，没有很多书可以读，但却有一大帮兄弟姐妹。可是，你现在过得不错，而且也比以前快乐，不是吗？"她问。这个人英俊、体面又富有。然而，任何人只要仔细观察，就会发现他的眼神充满着疲倦；不说话的时候，他的嘴角总是下垂，显得很伤感。

"我现在干得不错。非常感谢你的关心。"这个人爽朗地笑起来，"告诉我，你觉得我今天应该从你那儿买多少肥皂呢？"

"你姨妈家里现在还有多少肥皂没用掉？"经验老道的推销员有建设性地问，"她平时一般能用掉多少肥皂呢？"

"哦，我一点都不清楚。不过肥皂能存放很长时间，对吧？"

"我也不知道，不过我口袋里正好有本宣传册。可以帮你查查看。"丽贝卡一边老实地回答，一边从衣服口袋里掏出宣传册。

"推销肥皂能让你赚上不少钱，你打算用这笔钱干吗呢？"丽贝卡的顾客问。

"我们并不是为了自己才卖肥皂的，"丽贝卡向他倾诉，"我的朋友爱玛·简是铁匠的女儿，家境富裕。她现在牵着马在门外等候。她并不需要钱。我虽然很穷，可是跟姨妈住

any money. I am poor, but I live with my aunts in a brick house in town. They would not like to think of me as a door-to-door peddler. Emma Jane and I are only trying to help our friends, the Simpsons, win a prize. They are not nearly as well off as we are."

Rebecca had never thought of mentioning the circumstances of the Simpsons to her previous customers, but this gentleman had such patience and seemed to want to hear all about them. So she found herself describing the bad borrowing habits of Mr. Simpson, and the hardships endured by the Simpson family as a whole — their joyless life, their poverty, and their need of a *banquet* lamp with a crepe paper shade to brighten their existence.

"I have no doubt that the Simpsons would find this lamp useful," said the gentleman. "They should have it if they want it, especially since you and your friend are working so hard to help them get it. I've known what it was myself to do without a banquet lamp. Now, give me the order form, and let's do some calculations. How much do the Simpsons lack at this moment?"

"If they sell two hundred more bars total for this month and the next, they can have the lamp by Christmas," Rebecca answered. "With a hundred more, they can get the shade for it by next summer. But I'm afraid that I won't be able to sell much after today, because my Aunt Miranda may disapprove. Today

在镇上的那幢砖房里。她们不喜欢我做挨家挨户兜售的小贩。我和爱玛·简只是为了帮助我们的朋友辛普森家的孩子赢得奖品。他们可不像我们俩生活得那么好。"

丽贝卡从来没有想过要把辛普森家的情况告诉前面几位顾客，可是，这位绅士多么耐心，似乎想听完所有的事。因此，丽贝卡开始向他讲述辛普森先生不问自拿的坏毛病，辛普森一家的艰难处境——他们缺少快乐的生活、他们的贫困，还有他们急需一盏绉纱灯罩的宴会灯来照亮他们的生活。

"我非常肯定辛普森一家会发现这盏灯十分有用，"绅士说，"如果他们需要它，就该得到它，尤其是你和你的朋友为了帮助他们而这么努力地工作。我尝过没有宴会灯的滋味。现在，把订单给我，让我们来算一算。目前辛普森一家总共缺多少钱呢？"

"要是他们这个月和下个月多卖出两百条肥皂，那么圣诞节就能得到一盏灯。"丽贝卡回答，"再多卖掉一百条的话，明年夏天他们就可以给它添置一个灯罩。可是，我担心过了今天我就没法卖肥皂了，因为米兰达姨妈可能不会赞成我这么做。今天她不在家，没法征得她的同意。爱玛·简的

she wasn't home to ask. Mrs. Perkins, Emma Jane's mother, said that she supposed it would be all right, just for today."

"I see. Well, here's what we'll do. I will take three hundred bars today, and that will cover everything — lamp, shade, and all."

Rebecca's stool was dangerously near the edge of the porch. As she heard this fantastic proposal, she made a sudden movement, tipped over, and disappeared head first into a clump of lilac bushes. It was a very short distance to fall, fortunately. The amused philanthropist helped her up and set her on her feet again.

"You should never seem surprised when you have taken such a large order," he teased her with a smile. "You ought to have replied, "Can't you make it three hundred and fifty bars?" instead of falling off the porch in that unbusinesslike manner."

"I could never say anything so bold!" Rebecca exclaimed, *blushing* scarlet. "But it doesn't seem right for you to buy so much soap. Are you sure that you can afford it all?"

"If I can't, I'll save on something else."
"What if your aunt doesn't like this brand of soap?"
"My aunt always likes what I like."
"Mine never likes what I like!" Rebecca couldn't help exclaiming.

118

妈妈，也就是珀金太太说，她估计我只有今天能卖肥皂。"

"我懂了。好吧，一切看我们的。我今天就买下三百条肥皂，这笔钱可以换来所有的东西——宴会灯、灯罩，还有别的什么。"

丽贝卡坐的凳子就放在门廊边上，非常危险。当她听到绅士这番稀奇古怪的建议时，突然动了一下，结果整个人翻下门廊，头先着地，掉进了丁香花丛中。幸亏门廊离地面很近。这位慈善家乐呵呵地把她拉起来，重新让她坐到自己身边。

"当你获得这么一大笔订单的时候，你不应该表现得如此惊讶。"他面带微笑地取笑丽贝卡，"你该这么回答：'难道您不能买下三百五十条肥皂吗？'而不是这么没用地从门廊上摔下去。"

"我决不可能说出这么大胆的话！"丽贝卡红着脸叫起来，"可是，您没必要买下这么多肥皂啊。您确信您有钱买下所有的肥皂吗？"

"如果钱不够，我可以从其他地方省下来。"
"要是您的姨妈不喜欢这个牌子的肥皂该怎么办？"
"只要是我喜欢的，我姨妈都喜欢。"
"我姨妈从来都不喜欢我喜欢的东西！"丽贝卡忍不住叫起来。

"Then there's something wrong with your aunt!" the man replied.

"Or with me," said Rebecca, laughing.

"May I ask the name of my excellent and persuasive saleslady, so that I may remember it a decade later, when I'll no doubt need more soap?"

"Rebecca Rowena Randall, sir."

"What? All three? Your mother was generous with names. Would you like to know the name of your best customer to date?"

"I think I know already! I'm sure you must be Mr. Aladdin of the Arabian Nights. Mr. Aladdin of the magic lamp!"

"Well, you're not too far wrong. My name is Mr. Adam Ladd, at your service. Why don't we go tell Emma Jane that you two have sold out your supply of soap in one fell swoop?" he suggested.

Together they went back down the driveway, where Mr. Ladd lifted out the remaining cases of soap and then helped the two girls back onto the driver's seat of the wagon. They all agreed to arrange for the lamp to arrive as a surprise for the Simpsons on Thanksgiving Day. Then the two girls went on their way. As they left, they broke into another chorus of thanks and of good-byes, during which tears of joy welled up in Rebecca's eyes.

"Oh, don't mention it!" Mr. Ladd called out as the white

"那么，是你姨妈有问题！"这个男人回答说。

"或者是我不对。"丽贝卡笑着说。

"我可否有幸知道这位优秀的、有说服力的销售小姐的名字？这样，十年以后我需要更多肥皂的时候，还可能记得你。"

"我叫丽贝卡·罗威娜·兰德尔，先生。"

"什么？有三个字？你母亲给你取名真是大方啊。你想知道你目前为止遇上的最好的顾客的名字吗？"

"我想我已经知道啦！我敢说你肯定是《一千零一夜》里面的阿拉丁先生。拥有神灯的阿拉丁先生！"

"好吧，你猜得倒不怎么离谱。我的名字叫亚当·拉德，愿为您效劳。我们为什么不去告诉爱玛·简，就因为你摔了一跤，所以你们俩卖掉了所有的肥皂？"他提议。

于是，他们俩走下门廊，来到车道上，在那，拉德先生把剩余的肥皂箱搬下货车，然后帮助两个小女孩坐上驾驶座。他们一致同意订购一盏宴会灯，感恩节那天送到辛普森家里，给他们一个惊喜。然后，两个女孩就上路了。离开的时候，她们再三道谢，跟他告别，此时，丽贝卡的眼里充满着喜悦的泪水。

"哦，别客气！"拉德先生冲着她们大喊。此时，她们

horse pulled into the road. "I was a sort of traveling sales-man myself at one point, years ago. I like to see the thing well done. Good-bye, Miss Rebecca Rowena! Just let me know whenever you have anything else to sell, for I am cer-tain beforehand that I shall want the item in question!"

On Thanksgiving Day, the banquet lamp arrived in a large packing box. It was taken out and set up by Seesaw Simpson, who suddenly began to admire and respect the business abil-ity of his sisters and friends. Rebecca could see, from her own window in the brick house, the gorgeous trophy lit up and shining from the Simpsons' living-room window. All winter long, the banquet lamp sent a blaze of crimson glory through its red paper *shade* out into the darkness of snowy nights.

驾着白马来到大路上。"几年前，我也做过旅行推销员。我喜欢看见一切顺利。再见，丽贝卡·罗威娜小姐！下次有什么东西要卖的话提前告诉我一声，我肯定会买下它们。"

　　感恩节那天，辛普森家收到一个装有宴会灯的大包装箱。西索·辛普森把灯拿出来，放到桌上。突然，他对姐妹们和朋友们的推销能力产生了钦佩和敬意。丽贝卡从砖房卧室的窗口可以看见这件华丽的奖品被点亮了，它的光芒从辛普森家的客厅里放射出来。整个漫长的冬天，这盏灯透过红色的灯罩，散发出深红色的光芒，穿透雪夜的黑暗。

14

HIGH SCHOOL AT WAREHAM

Rebecca's fifteenth birthday had come and gone. She had outgrown the one-room schoolhouse in Riverboro, and had been sent to the senior high school in Wareham. Rebecca's intention was to complete the three-year course of study in two years, since her mother and aunts wanted her to be equipped to earn her own living by the time she reached the age of seventeen. She planned to earn money teaching, both to help pay the mortgage on Sunnybrook Farm, and to help with the education of her younger brothers and sisters back home.

Wareham was a pretty village, much larger than Riverboro, with a broad main street shaded by *maples* and elms. It had a pharmacy, a blacksmith's forge, a plumber, a dry-goods store, and several other shops, two churches, and a good number of boarding houses where students from out of town could find lodging. The high school was the center of cultural life in the village. There was only one such *establishment* in the county. Boys and girls from a wide array of surrounding towns and villages gathered in Wareham to learn a profession. These

十四

威尔汉姆高中

丽贝卡度过了她第十五个生日。可是，她已经长大了，不适合待在利佛保罗那个只有一间房子的学校了，被送到威尔汉姆高中继续求学。丽贝卡想在两年内完成三年的学业，因为她妈妈和姨妈想让她在十七岁就能自食其力。她打算今后以教书为生，一方面可以帮助偿还太阳溪农场的抵押贷款，另一方面还能供家里的弟弟妹妹上学。

威尔汉姆是一个漂亮的村庄，比利佛保罗大得多，宽阔的主街道两边种着枫树和榆树。村里有一家药房、一个铁匠铺、一家水管店、一个干货铺，还有一些其他的店铺、两座教堂和好几家住宿旅馆，外地来的学生可以在那寄宿。这所高中是村子里文化生活的中心。整个村子就这么一座学校。一拨一拨的男孩和女孩从附近的镇上和村里涌到威尔汉姆高中学习一技之长。这些学生来自各个阶层——有的家境富

students were of every type — wealthy, middle-class, and of relatively humble financial means, like Rebecca.

The school's dominance over the affairs of the town provided an opportunity for a great deal of foolish and reckless behavior. Surprisingly, students did not take advantage of their position to misbehave. There were also occasional bursts of silliness from flirtatious girls like Huldah Meserve. Her idea of fun was to have an ever-changing court of admiring boys to fetch and carry for her.

Huldah had the bad habit of bragging about the hearts she kept breaking to girls who did not have boyfriends. It did not take long for this to wreck the childhood friendship that had been established back in Riverboro among Huldah, Emma Jane, and Rebecca. Before the end of the first semester, Rebecca and Emma Jane had begun to sit at one end of the train going to and from Riverboro, while Huldah occupied the other end of the car with her court. Sometimes this company was brilliant beyond words, including a certain boy named Monte Cristo, who often spent money on a round-trip ticket simply to accompany Huldah to Riverboro before turning around and traveling back to Wareham on the next train.

Rebecca remained more or less indifferent to boys. They were good comrades, but counted for little else. She liked studying in the same classes and at the library with them. She also enjoyed working with them on the school newspaper. But she

裕,有的是中产阶级,还有的来自相对贫困的家庭,就像丽贝卡。

学校在村里的主导地位为滋生大量愚蠢的、不顾后果的行为提供了温床。然而令人惊讶的是,学生并没有因此而胡作非为。不过,偶尔也会有一些轻浮的女孩子做出愚蠢的事来,就像胡尔达·梅泽夫。她不断变换身边的追求者,把他们迷得团团转,并以此为乐。

胡尔达有个坏毛病,就是喜欢向那些没有男朋友的女孩子吹嘘自己伤了他们的心。这种行为很快就破坏了她和爱玛·简、丽贝卡三人从童年起就在利佛保罗建立起来的友谊。从第一个学期末开始,每次往返利佛保罗,丽贝卡和爱玛·简都坐到火车的一头,而胡尔达和她的追求者坐在另一头。有时候,她的追求者才华横溢,难以用言语形容,蒙特·克力斯托就是这样的人。他经常花钱买往返利佛保罗的车票,只是为了陪胡尔达回家,然后搭乘下一班火车回威尔汉姆。

丽贝卡对男孩子多少有些冷漠。他们是她的好伙伴,可是除此之外就没什么了。她喜欢和男孩子在同一个教室或图书馆一起学习。她还喜欢跟他们一起编校报。可是,她的理

was protected by her ideals and sense of dignity from the flirtatiousness that Huldah Meserve displayed on a daily basis.

Rebecca was principally interested in Wareham's high school for the education that was offered there. She admired one teacher above all others — Miss Maxwell, who taught English literature and composition. It was rumored that Miss Maxwell "wrote", which meant that she had published stories and essays in magazines. This height of achievement made Rebecca somewhat shy around her favorite teacher. However, she sought by every means in her power to remain, by far, the best and most interesting student in all of Miss Maxwell's classes.

After just one year of course work, Rebecca was granted a great privilege. On Fridays, from three until four-thirty in the afternoon, she was allowed to consult Miss Maxwell's collection of books, which lined two entire walls of her parlor. Every Friday for the following year, Rebecca sat in a big armchair in Miss Maxwell's parlor and read to her heart's content — poetry, biographies, novels, essays, great volumes of history and philosophy — choosing whatever she liked on any given Friday. At four-thirty. Miss Maxwell would come home from class to engage in a precious half-hour of conversation before Rebecca had to catch the train to Riverboro, where she spent every weekend helping her aunts catch up with household chores, laundry, and mending.

想和自尊使她远离轻浮的调情,这种轻浮的举止胡尔达·梅泽夫每天都在上演。

丽贝卡的兴趣主要放在威尔汉姆高中的教育上。在所有老师中,她最崇拜一位老师——麦克斯韦小姐,她教英国文学和写作课。大家都在传麦克斯韦小姐会"写作",说的是她在杂志上发表过小说和随笔。这番成就使丽贝卡在喜爱的老师身边感到有些害羞。然而,她竭尽所能在麦克斯韦小姐开的所有课上成为最优秀、最好学的学生。

经过一年的课程学习之后,丽贝卡获得特许。每个星期五下午三点到四点半,她可以翻阅麦克斯韦小姐的藏书,她家客厅里整整摆满两墙的书。第二年每个星期五下午,丽贝卡坐在麦克斯韦小姐家客厅里的大扶手椅上,心满意足地阅读——诗歌、传记、小说、随笔、成卷的历史和哲学书——每个星期五她都可以选择任何一本她想看的书。四点半的时候,麦克斯韦小姐从教室回到家,赶在丽贝卡坐火车回利佛保罗前,利用半个小时的宝贵时间与她交谈。丽贝卡每个周末都回利佛保罗,帮助姨妈干家务、洗衣服、做针线活。

Late one afternoon in her senior year, Rebecca was reading David Copperfield when she happened to look up and see, through the window, two figures coming down the path to Miss Maxwell's house. It was Adam Ladd and Huldah Meserve. Huldah seemed to be flirting outrageously with Mr. Ladd as she picked her way through the snow in dainty black boots. Rebecca was surprised at how jealous she felt.

In the years that had passed since Rebecca fell off Mr. Ladd's porch, she had gradually come to know and like her soap sponsor. She had discovered, much to her surprise, that he was a very influential man, with controlling interests in railroads and other large businesses in the region. He was even on the board of trustees for Wareham's high school! Yet he was a man of only thirty years, not at all middle-aged, as she had thought back when she was a child of fourteen. Rebecca was astonished to realize all at once that she could not bear to give up her share of Adam Ladd's friendship to Huldah — Huldah, so pretty and saucy, and so attentive!

　　丽贝卡读高年级时，有一天下午很晚的时候，她正在看《大卫·科波菲尔》。她无意中抬起头，看见窗外有两个人沿着小路朝麦克斯韦小姐家走来。那是亚当·拉德和胡尔达·梅泽夫。胡尔达专挑雪地上走，露出漂亮的黑靴子，似乎在向拉德先生调情。此时，丽贝卡对自己的忌妒心感到十分惊讶。

　　自从丽贝卡在拉德先生家的门廊前摔了一跤后，这些年来，她开始渐渐了解拉德先生，并且喜欢上这个肥皂赞助者。令她吃惊的是，她发现拉德先生是个非常有权势的人。他在这个地区投资铁路和其他大型事业。他甚至是威尔汉姆高中校董会的成员！然而，他才三十岁，还没到中年。丽贝卡回想起那时自己十四岁。她突然惊讶地意识到自己无法放弃与拉德先生的友谊，把它拱手让给胡尔达——她是那么漂亮、那么迷人！

15

A CHERISHED PHOTO

Rebecca watched Huldah and Mr. Ladd part company at Miss Maxwell's gate. Huldah waved good-bye with a toss of her *gorgeous* red hair and continued on her way. Suddenly, the door to the parlor opened, and Mr. Ladd stood before the startled and *flustered* Rebecca.

"Miss Maxwell informed me that I might find Miss Rebecca Rowena Randall here reading, as is her custom on Friday afternoons," he joked with a sweeping, gentlemanly bow in her direction. "There is a meeting of railway directors in Portland tomorrow, and I thought that I'd stop off in Wareham today to visit the school and to give my oh-so-valuable advice concerning its affairs, both educational and financial."

"I still can't get used to the fact that you're a trustee here," Rebecca said. "You seem to make light of the power you have. But I know that you're very interested in the school and that you do give very sound advice concerning its affairs — both educational and financial."

十五

一张珍藏的相片

丽贝卡看着拉德先生和胡尔达在麦克斯韦小姐家门前分手。胡尔达向他挥手告别，然后甩了甩那头鲜艳的红头发，继续上路。突然，客厅的门打开了，拉德先生出现在惊慌失措的丽贝卡面前。

"麦克斯韦小姐告诉我，或许可以在这里找到丽贝卡·罗威娜·兰德尔小姐，星期五下午她都会在这里看书。"他开玩笑说，朝丽贝卡彬彬有礼地鞠了个躬。"明天波特兰有一个铁路股东大会，我想我今天可以顺道拜访一下威尔汉姆高中，对学校的教育和财政提出非常有价值的建议。"

"我仍然不敢相信你会是这里的董事。"丽贝卡说，"你好像不太在意自己拥有的权力。不过，我知道你对学校很感兴趣，而且你确实对学校事务——教育和财政——提出了合理的意见。"

"You are remarkably wise and intelligent for your seventeen years," Mr. Ladd said as he settled into a chair by the fire. "The fact is, I accepted the trusteeship in memory of my mother, whose happiest years were spent here. She died when I was eight. The school might have existed for twenty or twenty-five years at that point. Would you like to see a picture of her?"

Rebecca took the leather case that Mr. Ladd pulled from the breast pocket of his jacket, where he kept it close to his heart. She opened it to find an innocent, pink-and-white daisy of a face, so open and sensitive that the vision of it went straight to Rebecca's heart.

"Oh, what a sweet, lovely flower she must have been!" Rebecca exclaimed, tears filling her eyes.

"The flower had to bear all sorts of storms," Adam Ladd said gravely. "The bitter weather of the world bowed its head and dragged it to the earth. I was only a child at the time. I could do nothing to protect her, and there was no one else to keep trouble at bay. Now I have success and money and power, everything that would have kept her alive and happy, but it is too late. All that has come to me seems so useless sometimes, since I cannot share it with her!"

Rebecca had never seen this side of Adam Ladd before. Her heart reached out to him in sympathy and understanding. "I'm so glad that you told me, and that you showed me her photo, so

134

"就你十七岁的年龄来说,你非常聪明、机智。"拉德先生坐到炉火边的椅子上,说,"事实上,我之所以接受董事一职是为了纪念我的母亲,她最快乐的几年是在这里度过的。她在我八岁时就去世了。那个时候,学校大概创立了二十或二十五年。你想看看她的相片吗?"

丽贝卡从拉德先生手里接过一个皮盒子,它原本放在拉德先生的上衣口袋里,紧贴着他的胸口。丽贝卡打开盒子,发现相片上是一张白里透红的雏菊般纯真的脸,如此率真、如此敏感,第一眼就打动了丽贝卡的心。

"哦,她以前该是多么娇艳、可爱的花朵啊!"丽贝卡热泪盈眶地说。

"这朵花不得不经受各种风暴,"亚当·拉德沉重地说,"世上恶劣的气候让她抬不起头来,把她拽倒在地。那时我还是个孩子。我没法保护她,也没有人助她度过难关。现在我成功了,有钱有势,可以做任何让她快乐的事,不过已经太迟了。有时候,这一切对我来说简直毫无意义,因为我没法与她分享所有的一切!"

丽贝卡从来没有见过拉德先生的这一面。她心中对他充满了同情和理解。"我真高兴您能告诉我您母亲的事,并且给我看她的相片,这样我就可以记住她了。真希望她能够活

that I can remember her. I wish that she could have lived to see you grow up so strong and good. My mother is always sad and busy. But once, when she looked at my brother John, I heard her say, 'My children make up for everything.' That's what your mother would have thought about you — I'm sure of it."

"You are such a comfort to me, Rebecca," Adam said as he rose from his chair to leave. "What am I going to do when you leave this place, when you've become a schoolteacher in stylish suits in some faraway place? You'll have no time for me anymore. Please don't give me up until you have to!"

"Oh, I won't, Mr. Ladd, I can promise you that. Our friendship is bound to last a long, long time," Rebecca replied as she shook Adam's hand good-bye.

"By the way," Adam said as he stood in the doorway, "who is that young girl with all that pretty red hair and such sophisticated manners? She escorted me down the path on my way here to see you. Do you know whom I mean?"

"It must have been Huldah Meserve," Rebecca said in a voice that she hoped sounded calm and neutral. "She is from Riverboro and will graduate next year. She used to be a close friend of mine."

Adam looked into Rebecca's eyes, so friendly and sincere. He remembered his trip along the path with Huldah and how

着看见您长成这么强壮、这么好的人。我妈妈成天忙个不停，而且总是很忧伤。不过有一次，她看着我的兄弟约翰，我听见她说：'为了我的孩子，做什么都值了。'您的母亲也是这么认为的——我敢肯定。"

"丽贝卡，你真会安慰我。"拉德起身离开时，说，"等你离开学校到遥远的地方去，穿上时髦的衣服成为一名教师，那时我该怎么办？你再也没时间留给我了。不到万不得已，请别抛弃我！"

"哦，我不会的，拉德先生，我可以向你保证。我们的友谊一定会天长地久。"丽贝卡跟拉德先生握手道别时说。

"顺便问一句，"拉德先生站在门口，问，"那个长着漂亮的红头发、举止老练的姑娘是谁？她陪着我一路走到这儿来见你。你知道我说的是谁吗？"

"一定是胡尔达·梅泽夫。"丽贝卡说。她希望自己的声音听起来镇定、不带感情色彩。"她从利佛保罗来这儿念书，明年毕业。她曾经是我的好朋友。"

亚当真诚、友善地看着丽贝卡的眼睛。他想起刚才来时的路上，胡尔达多么明显地跟他调情。然后，他用最严肃、

she had flirted with him so obviously. He then said in the most serious and genuinely affectionate way possible, "Don't pattern yourself after Huldah, Rebecca. Clover blossoms that grow in the fields of Sunnybrook Farm may not appear beautiful next to gaudy sunflowers, but clover is sweet and wholesome, and ultimately much more beautiful."

With these words, and blushing slightly at the rather new and sudden vision he had of Rebecca as a young woman, Adam Ladd took his leave of her.

最真诚的口气说："丽贝卡，不要学胡尔达的样。生长在太阳溪农场的三叶草可能不如艳丽的向日葵那么漂亮；可是，甜美、健康的三叶草最终还是会胜过向日葵。"

说完这番话，亚当·拉德向丽贝卡告别。此时，他第一次突然意识到丽贝卡已经长成大姑娘了，脸上不觉微微泛红。

139

16

GRADUATION DAY

At last, the great day dawned for Rebecca — the day to which she had been looking forward for two years. It was the first goal to be reached on her journey toward *independence* as an adult. School days were now at an end; graduation day was at hand. It was, even now, being heralded by the sun rising in the eastern sky over Wareham.

Anyone who is unacquainted with life in the country could not imagine the importance of graduation day in a small rural *community*. In the matter of preparation, wealth of organizational detail, and sheer excitement, it far surpasses a wedding.

Wareham was shaken to its very center oh this day of days. Mothers and fathers of all the scholars, and relatives from the remotest corners of the region, had come by train and coach and farm wagon into town. Former pupils of the high school streamed back into the dear old village, the site of so many memorable events. Lines of buggies and wagons were

十六

毕业那天

对丽贝卡来说，重要的日子终于来临了——这一天她已经盼了整整两年。这是她即将实现的第一个人生目标：作为成人走向独立。现在，学校生活就要结束，毕业典礼近在眼前。威尔汉姆东边的天际升起了一轮旭日，预示着美好的开始。

不熟悉乡村生活的人没法想象毕业典礼在村里的重要性。就事前的准备工作、大量的组织细节和激动的心情而言，它远胜于一场婚礼。

在这一天，威尔汉姆镇上的人都会聚到这所高中。毕业生的父母亲，还有亲戚从最偏远的角落坐火车或四轮马车或农用的货车赶来威尔汉姆。以前从这所高中毕业的学生也纷纷涌向这座亲爱又古老的村庄，这里有许多美好的回忆。一排排轻便马车和货车停在通往小镇的林荫道两旁，拉车的马悠闲地甩着尾巴。大街上到处都是穿戴时髦的人。时髦不仅

parked along both sides of the shady roads leading into town, the horses swishing their tails in *luxurious* idleness. The streets were filled with people wearing their best clothes. The fashions included not only the latest styles, but also the well-preserved costumes of previous generations. There were all sorts and conditions of men and women — storekeepers, lawyers, doctors, shoemakers, professors, ministers, farmers — because their children all attended high school together.

The graduates, especially the young women among them, were dressed with a completeness of detail that practically defied reason and common sense. Dotted or plain Swiss-muslin dresses were the favorite costume, but there were a few girls who perspired in white cashmere, because such dresses were thought to be useful during other seasons. Blue and pink waist ribbons fluttered in the June breeze.

Rebecca had known, early on, that her mother would be too burdened with farmwork to attend the ceremony. She had also realized that her aunts could not afford to buy material for a special graduation dress. So she and Emma Jane had explored Emma Jane's attic, where they found a great deal of white butter muslin, often called cheesecloth. It was commonly used to strain preserves during jelly-making season. They decided that the material, although not usually employed for making dresses, would just have to do in a pinch.

指当下最流行的款式，也指过去流行的依旧保存完好的样式。这些男男女女从事各种行业——店主、律师、医生、鞋匠、教授、牧师、农民——因为他们的孩子都在同一所高中上学。

　　毕业生，尤其是他们中间年轻的女学生，穿着别出心裁，超乎人们的想象。有圆点或单色的薄细布做成的衣服深受她们的喜爱，可是，也有少数几个女孩子穿着白色羊绒衫，因为这种衣服也适合在别的季节穿。系在腰间蓝粉相间的丝带，在六月的微风中飘舞。

　　丽贝卡早就知道农场上的活儿太多，妈妈抽不开身过来参加她的毕业典礼。她也清楚姨妈没钱买新的布料，为她特地缝制毕业典礼上穿的衣服。所以她和爱玛·简在爱玛家的阁楼里东找西找，终于发现许多白色的奶油包布①，通常叫做干酪包布②。做果冻的时候，常用这种布来保存果冻。尽管人们不太用它来做衣服，不过她们决定必要时用上它。

① 一种无浆的稀薄布，原用来包裹黄油。
② 一种薄纱织物，原用作包干酪、黄油等之用，现也用来制作衣服、窗帘等。

Emma Jane could have afforded dotted Swiss muslin instead, but she decided to follow her friend in cheesecloth as she had stood by her through other trials and tribulations. The stitches that went into pleating and tucking the inexpensive material, worth only three or four pennies per yard, made the dresses altogether lovely. Rebecca and Emma Jane could have given sewing lessons to their classmates who were dressed in silks and other expensive materials.

The class of which Rebecca was president was not likely to follow tradition. Instead of marching two-by-two from the high school to the church, the graduating students, under Rebecca's leadership, had chosen to proceed on a sort of royal chariot. A hay cart had been decorated with fireen vines and bunches of daisies. Every inch of the cart was covered in greenery. Two white horses pulled the improvised chariot. Seated on maple boughs, the girls from Rebecca's graduating class waved to the assembled crowds. The boys marched behind the vehicle.

Rebecca drove the cart, seated on a greenery-covered bench that looked somewhat like a throne for a fairy princess. Tall and slender, her dark hair braided into a crown on her head, the fire of youthful joy in her face, Rebecca seemed like a young muse or wood nymph. The flowery hay cart, with its freight of blooming girlhood, looked like an allegorical painting depicting "The Morning of Life".

爱玛·简原本有钱买有圆点的薄细布，可是她决定跟她的朋友一样，用这种薄纱做衣服，因为她们一起经历了许多考验和磨难。她们用一针一线把廉价的布料缝制成漂亮的衣服，而这种布料每码只要三到四便士。丽贝卡和爱玛·简可以给班上那些穿着丝绸和其他昂贵面料衣服的同学上缝纫课了。

丽贝卡所在的毕业班不想遵循惯例。毕业生都是两个两个从学校走到教堂，可是在丽贝卡的带领下，她班上的毕业生选择坐在华丽的马车上行进。他们用绿色的葡萄藤和一束束雏菊装点这辆运干草的货车。货车上每一寸都被绿意覆盖着。两匹白马来拉这辆临时布置的马车。丽贝卡班上的女生坐在横着枫树枝的车上，一路向围观的人群挥手。男孩子们跟在马车后面行进。

丽贝卡坐在布满绿意的驾驶座上赶车，这个位子有点像漂亮公主的宝座。丽贝卡身材高挑，乌黑的长发在头顶盘成王冠状，脸上流露出喜悦的青春的火花。此时，丽贝卡看上去就像年轻的缪斯女神或林泽女神。运干草的货车缀满鲜花，还有满满一车含苞待放的少女，这情景就像一幅描绘"生命之晨"的油画，意味深长。

The people gathered for the ceremony applauded and cheered as the chariot of graduates drove past. Proud parents and friends did not stop applauding and cheering during the actual ceremony, either, although the principal tried to keep his mood serious to match the ostensible gravity of the occasion.

During the ceremony, Rebecca was awarded a prize of fifty dollars for an essay she had written, entitled "The Rose of Joy". At the announcement of the prize, Jeremiah Cobb jumped up and cheered until he was hoarse. Mrs. Cobb was glad that they were seated near the back of the church, because her husband made a spectacle of himself in his enthusiasm for Rebecca's fine achievement.

When the diplomas were presented, all students came forward in turn to claim their roll of parchment from the principal, acknowledging him with a bow that had been the subject of anxious thought and practice for weeks. Rounds of applause greeted each graduate at this thrilling moment. Mr. Cobb's behavior when Rebeccca came forward became even more flamboyant. His clapping and stomping made for a week's worth of gossip in both Wareham and Riverboro. Old Mrs. Webb claimed that, during two hours of his antics, Jeremiah Cobb had simply worn out her pew — carpet, cushions, and woodwork — worn it out more than she had by sitting in it for forty years!

当毕业生的马车经过时，参加典礼的人鼓起掌来，发出阵阵欢呼声。尽管在这庄严的场合校长极力克制激动的心情，想要保持严肃，可是自豪的父母和朋友却不停地鼓掌、欢呼。

在毕业典礼上，丽贝卡获得五十美元的奖金，因为她写了一篇名为《玫瑰的欢乐》的随笔。颁奖的时候，杰里迈亚·科布从人群中跳了出来，为丽贝卡欢呼，直到声嘶力竭。科布太太很高兴他们坐在教堂后面，因为她丈夫在众人面前为丽贝卡取得的成绩激动不已，成为一道奇观。

颁发毕业证书的时候，所有的毕业生轮流走上前，从校长手中接过证书，并向他鞠躬致谢。为此，在过去的几个星期里，练习鞠躬成了他们的头等大事。在那激动人心的时刻，每个学生都迎来了一阵掌声。当丽贝卡走上前领取证书时，科布先生的行为更是离谱。他又是拍手又是跺脚，结果在之后的一个星期，他成了威尔汉姆和利佛保罗居民茶余饭后的谈资。上了年纪的韦伯太太声称，在那两个小时里，杰里迈亚·科布坐坏了她的靠背长凳——毯子、坐座垫和木架——她在这个位子上坐了四十年都没有破坏得这么严重！

After the ceremony, Mr. Cobb and Mr. Ladd encountered one another during the reception. They had a lively conversation about Rebecca, both of them bursting with love and pride.

"I suppose up in Boston, girls as pretty and as accomplished as Rebecca are as thick as blackberries on the bush?" asked Mr. Cobb, beaming and nodding in the direction where Rebecca was standing with Emma Jane, talking to Mrs. Cobb.

"There may well be such young ladies," smiled Mr. Ladd, noting the old man's mood, "but I don't happen to know of any who compare more favorably."

"My eyesight's so poor," Mr. Cobb confessed. "That's probably why she looked to me to be the most beautiful girl up on that platform."

"There's no failure in my eyes," Mr. Ladd replied. "That's just how she looked to me. You manage to see quite well, in fact — I wouldn't go to the eye doctor just yet."

"What did you think of her voice when they all sang those choruses? Anything special about it? I'm no judge of these matters," admitted Mr. Cobb.

"Her voice made the others sound poor and thin by comparison, I thought," was Adam Ladd's reply.

"Well, I'm glad to hear your opinion, you being a well-traveled young man and all that," said Mr. Cobb. "Mrs. Cobb

148

毕业典礼结束以后，科布先生和拉德先生在招待会上不期而遇。他们愉快地谈起丽贝卡，两个人都对丽贝卡充满了爱意，为她感到骄傲。

"我想，在波士顿，像丽贝卡这么漂亮、这么有才华的姑娘是否跟灌木丛中的黑梅一样多？"科布先生问，他朝丽贝卡点头微笑。这时，丽贝卡与爱玛·简站在一起，正在跟科布太太聊天。

"或许有很多这样的姑娘，"拉德先生笑着说，留心这位老人的情绪。"可是，我不知道还有谁比她更讨人喜欢。"

"我的眼睛不太好使，"科布先生说，"大概这就是为什么我觉得她是讲台上最漂亮的姑娘。"

"我的眼睛没什么毛病，"拉德先生回答说，"她也是我眼中最漂亮的姑娘。事实上，你千方百计想要看得仔细些——而我恰好不需要看眼科医生。"

"她们合唱的时候，你觉得她的嗓子怎么样？有什么特别的地方吗？我对这些不太懂。"科布先生说。

"我认为，其他姑娘们的嗓音与她相比显得单薄、无力。"拉德回答。

"好吧，我很高兴听到你的看法。你是一个见多识广的年轻人。"科布先生说，"科布太太说，从我第一天赶车送她

149

says that I'm foolish about Rebecca and have been since the first day I drove her to Riverboro. My wife scolds me for spoiling her, but she spoils her as much as I do. Mercy! It just makes me sick at heart, thinking of all those parents of those other graduates traveling all this way to see their children graduate, and then having to compare them with Rebecca once they got here. Well, it sure was nice talking to you, Mr. Ladd. Come visit us in Riverboro some time soon."

"I'll plan on it at the first opportunity, Mr. Cobb!" Adam said heartily as he shook the hand of Rebecca's other admirer.

As Mr. Cobb walked away, Adam turned and once again admired Rebecca. He remembered their first meeting when she was fourteen, and marveled at how much she had grown. The smart and sassy girl who had once sold him soap was now a sophisticated young woman, ready to take on the world with zest, enthusiasm, and a kind heart.

去利佛保罗，就对丽贝卡盲目夸赞。老婆责备我溺爱丽贝卡，可是，她自己也像我一样宠她。天可怜见！一想到其他毕业生的父母不辞辛劳赶来观看孩子的毕业典礼，然后拿自己的孩子与丽贝卡比较，我就感到难过。拉德先生，真高兴跟你聊天。以后有时间来利佛保罗看我们。"

"科布先生，一有机会我就来拜访你们！"拉德先生与丽贝卡的另一个仰慕者握手告别的时候，热忱地说。

科布先生走开后，拉德先生转过身，再次欣赏丽贝卡。他记得两人初次见面时丽贝卡才十四岁，现在惊奇地发现她已经长大成人了。这个聪明又冒失的姑娘曾经向他推销肥皂，如今已长成干练的年轻女子，正满怀热心、激情和善心步入社会。

151

17

LOOKING TOWARD THE FUTURE

M rs. Cobb had come to the graduation ceremony with a troubling piece of news in her heart. She waited until the end of the celebration to break the news to Rebecca.

"I don't quite know how to tell you this, my sweet Rebecca. I wanted this day to be perfect for you. We're all so very proud of your accomplishments, of the person you have made of yourself. I wanted you to have all the happiness and fun you so richly deserve today," Mrs. Cobb began, struggling mightily with what she had to tell Rebecca.

"What's the matter? It's about my aunts, isn't it? Are they ill? I haven't yet seen them today!" Rebecca was begining to panic.

"Your Aunt Miranda had a bad stroke this morning when she and Jane were getting ready to drive over to Wareham

十七

期待未来

科布太太来参加毕业典礼的时候,心里藏着一个不幸的消息。她一直等到毕业典礼结束后才告诉丽贝卡。

"亲爱的丽贝卡,我不知道该如何对你开口。我想让今天成为你美好的一天。我们都对你取得的成绩和你的为人引以为傲。我想让你今天成为最快乐的姑娘,而且你也配享受这份快乐。"科布太太开始说话,内心激烈地斗争着该如何告诉丽贝卡。

"发生什么事啦?是关于我姨妈的,对不对?她们生病了吗?我今天还没有看见她们呢!"丽贝卡开始惊慌起来。

"你米兰达姨妈今天早上中风了,那时她和简准备停当,正要驾车来威尔汉姆参加你的毕业典礼。"科布太太说,"简

for your ceremony," said Mrs. Cobb. "Jane said that we weren't to let you know anything about it until the exercises were all over. She made me promise to make it seem like a normal day, a day of celebration. I'm sorry I kept it a secret from you, but I had to do it. Jane insisted that we do it this way."

"Let me get my things, and I'll go home with you this instant!" Rebecca exclaimed. "I just have to run and tell Miss Maxwell. She and I were supposed to visit the school in Edgewood, where I'm scheduled to begin teaching this fall. Poor Aunt Miranda! And I have been so happy today, so unthinkingly happy!"

"There's no harm in being happy, love. That's the way Jane wanted you to feel today. Emma Jane can help you pack your trunk and get your room in order before we leave. Jeremiah will drive you home in the coach, just like old times."

When Rebecca arrived home, it was after dark. The door to Miranda's sickroom was open. Rebecca entered quietly, clutching the daisies she had brought home as a gift. Miranda's pale, sharp face looked very tired on the pillow. Her body was pitifully still under the blankets of her bed.

"Come in," Miranda said, turning her eyes on her niece. "Don't mess up the bed with those flowers, now."

"Certainly not. Aunt Miranda! They're going to fit nicely

说，在毕业典礼结束之前我们不想让你知道这件事。她让我发誓，装作什么事都没有发生过，今天是庆祝的好日子。很抱歉我一直瞒着你，可是，我不得不这么做。简坚持要我们这么做。"

"我去收拾一下，马上就跟你们回家！"丽贝卡说，"我得跑去告诉麦克斯韦小姐一声。我们原想去布伦瑞克当地的学校看看，我打算今年秋天去那儿教书。可怜的米兰达姨妈！我今天太高兴了，简直难以想象！"

"亲爱的，你高兴并没有错。那正是简希望的。在我们离开之前，爱玛·简可以帮你整理行李和房间。杰里迈亚会赶车送你回家，就像以前一样。"

丽贝卡回到家时，天已经黑了。米兰达的病房门还开着。丽贝卡轻轻地走进去，手里拽着带回来的雏菊，准备送给米兰达姨妈。米兰达的头靠在枕头上，苍白、消瘦的脸看上去非常疲倦。她静静地躺在床上，可怜的身子蜷缩在毛毯下面。

"进来，"米兰达两眼转向侄女，说，"别让这些花弄乱了我的床。"

"当然不会，米兰达姨妈！它们插在这个玻璃瓶里刚刚

in this glass pitcher" said Rebecca, turning to the *washstand* as she tried to control her voice and stop the tears that had sprung to her eyes.

"Let me look at you. Come closer! What dress are you wearing?" demanded the invalid, trying to move her stiffened body so she could see better.

"My graduation dress, darling aunt," Rebecca replied softly. She sat down by the bedside and timidly touched her aunt's hand. Her heart swelled with tenderness at the sight of Miranda's drawn, pain-filled face.

"I am dreadfully ashamed to have you graduate in cheesecloth, Rebecca, but we just couldn't afford to spend money on new dress material. I'll try to make it up to you someday. I'm afraid you must have been the laughingstock of the whole high school!"

"It's all right. Aunt Miranda. Don't trouble yourself about me at all. Ever so many people said that our dresses were the very prettiest. They looked just like they were made of soft lace. I don't want you to worry about anything at all. Here I am, all grown up and graduated — number three in a class of twenty-two. Aunt Miranda! I've had a good teaching position offered to me already, at the Edgewood School. I'll be close enough to stay here nights and on the weekends, to help you and Aunt Jane."

好。"丽贝卡说着背过身，朝向洗脸盆，极力控制自己不失声，拼命忍住眼泪不往下流。

"让我看看你。走近些！你穿什么衣服？"病人问。她想移动僵硬的身子，以便能够看得清楚些。

"亲爱的姨妈，这是我的毕业礼服。"丽贝卡温柔地说。她坐在床边，胆怯地抚摸姨妈的手。看到米兰达因痛苦而扭曲的脸，丽贝卡心里充满着柔情。

"丽贝卡，让你穿薄纱做的衣服参加毕业典礼我真感到羞愧。可是，我们没钱买布料做新衣服。总有一天，我会给你做一件的。我担心你肯定成了全校师生的笑柄。"

"没关系，米兰达姨妈。别为我操心。很多很多人都说我们的衣服是最漂亮的。它们看上去就像用柔软的蕾丝做成的。我不想让您事事操心。现在，我已经长大成人而且毕业了——米兰达姨妈，全班二十二个人中我排名第三！我已经收到一份来自布伦瑞克学校的聘任书。学校离这里很近，我可以晚上和周末回家帮助您和简姨妈干活。"

There was a long pause, as Miranda struggled with her fatigue. "You listen to me," she said when she had the strength. "You do what you need to do for yourself and for your family. Your mother comes first, *regardless* of my sickness. I'd like to live long enough to know that you've paid off that mortgage on the farm, but I guess I won't last that long. Now, go and get your Aunt Jane. I need to speak to her a minute."

Here Miranda ceased speaking abruptly, having talked more than she knew was wise. Rebecca kissed Miranda on the forehead, whispered that she loved her, and crept from the room. By the time Jane entered, Miranda had fallen asleep. Jane waited until the next day, when she brought toast and tea to the sickroom, to remind her elder sister about the summons.

"I need to settle the future, before I go, Jane," Miranda began firmly to speak her mind. "There are things I need to talk over with you. We need to get everything worked out now, rather than later. So don't interrupt, and don't tell me I've got time, yet, because I'm not sure I do. When I'm dead and buried, I want you to bring Aurelia and the children down here to the brick house. I've put the house in Rebecca's name in my will, so she'll inherit it. I know that she'll want you to stay here, even once she's married. Try to get Aurelia to sell that worthless farm — it's not worth the interest on the mortgage that she's been paying all these years."

米兰达十分疲惫，谈话中止了一会儿。"听我说，"米兰达缓过劲来后说，"为你自己和你的家人做你该做的事。你妈妈不管我的病情，第一个过来看望我。我真想活着看你还清农场的抵押贷款，可是，我想我活不了那么久。现在，去把你简姨妈叫来。我要跟她聊几句。"

米兰达突然停下来，她知道自己已经说得太多了。丽贝卡亲了亲米兰达的前额，轻声表达对她的爱意，然后蹑手蹑脚地走出病房。简进来的时候，米兰达已经睡着了。简一直等到第二天她醒来。她端着烤面包和茶走进病房，暗示姐姐打起精神。

"简，在我走之前得安排一下身后事。"米兰达开始坚定地说，"有些事我得跟你谈谈。从现在起，我们需要让一切运作起来，而不是等到以后。所以不要打断我说话，也别提醒我时间到了，因为我也不敢肯定自己能否说完。等我死了，埋葬以后，我想让你把奥里莉亚和她的孩子们接到砖房来。我在遗嘱里把这座房子写上丽贝卡的名字，她将继承这幢砖房。我知道她想让你继续住在这儿，就算她以后结婚也一样。想办法让奥里莉亚卖掉那个一文不值的农场——这些年来它连偿还抵押贷款的利息都不够。"

"I think there's a good possibility that Adam Ladd plans to buy that land for the new railroad he's building," Jane said gently. "He's willing to pay six thousand dollars for it — much more than it's worth. That'll give all of us a good income. So don't you fret about money anymore, Miranda. We'll all be all right."

"Well, I will admit that that piece of news takes a load off my mind. That Adam Ladd is a really nice fellow, if you ask me. A fool to sink that kind of money into that Sunnybrook Farm of Rebecca's, but a thoughtful, generous soul all the same. Now, if you'll draw the curtains, I think I'll try to nap a little while." Miranda closed her eyes, a smile playing on her lips for the first time in weeks. She could seek peace, now that her affairs were settled for the good of all, especially for her niece Rebecca, of whom she had grown rather fond over the years they had spent together.

　　"我想，亚当·拉德很有可能买下那块土地，用来修建铁路。"简轻轻地说，"他乐意出六千美元买下它——这远远超过农场本身的价值。那会给我们带来一笔可观的收入。所以，米兰达，你不用再为钱而发愁。我们会过得很好。"

　　"好吧，我承认这个消息让我轻松不少。要是你问我亚当·拉德这人怎么样，我觉得他确实是个不错的家伙。这个傻瓜把一大笔钱扔在丽贝卡的太阳溪农场上，可是，他仍然有一颗体贴、慷慨的心。现在，要是你拉上窗帘，我想睡一会儿。"米兰达闭上眼睛，几个星期以来嘴角第一次露出笑容，她现在可以安息了。她的身后事已经安排妥当，尤其是她的侄女丽贝卡。在一起度过的几年里，米兰达已经变得越来越喜欢丽贝卡了。

词 汇 表

1

stagecoach ['steidʒkəutʃ] *n.* （旧时的）驿站马车；公共马车
constitute [kɔnstitju:t] *v.* 是；被算作
nightgown ['naitgaun] *n.* 睡衣

2

rumble [rʌmbl] *n.* 隆隆声
protest ['prəutest] *v.* 反对；抗议
brilliant [briliət] *adj.* 明亮的；鲜艳的

3

volunteer [vɔlən'tiə] *v.* 自愿做；义务做

4

obedient [ə'bi:diənt] *adj.* 顺从的
multiplication [,mʌltiplikeiʃən] *n.* 乘法
mortgage ['mɔ:gidʒ] *n.* 抵押

5

passionately ['pæʃənitli] *adj.* 热情的；有激情的
miserable ['mizərəbl] *adj.* 悲惨的；不幸的
desperate ['despərit] *adj.* 极度的；非常的

6

glint ['glint] v. 闪耀；闪烁
dazzling [dæzliŋ] adj. 灿烂的
gingham [giŋəm] n. 格子棉布

7

cherish ['tʃeriʃ] v. 珍爱；钟爱
triumph ['traiʌmf] n. 重大成就；伟大胜利

8

scold ['skəuld] v. 训词；责骂
impertinent [im'pə:tinənt] adj. 粗鲁无礼的
charitable ['tʃærətəbl] adj. 仁爱的；宽厚的

9

pinch [pintʃ] v. 捏住；夹紧
dawn [dɔ:n] v. 变得明朗
hint [hint] n 征兆；迹象

10

dignity ['dignəti] n. 自尊；自豪
sob [sɔb] n. 抽噎；啜泣

11

thanksgiving [θæŋks'giviŋ] n. 感谢；感恩节
gloomy ['glu:mi] adj. 黑暗的；阴沉的；令人沮丧的
ambitious [æm'biʃəns] adj. 有雄心的；野心勃勃的

12

glorious ['glɔːriəs] *adj.* 光荣的，显赫的
sparkling ['spaːkliŋ] *adj.* 闪烁的，闪闪发光的，发泡的
cider ['saidə] *n.* 苹果酒

13

sympathy ['simpəθi] *n.* 同情，同情心
banquet ['bæŋkwit] *n.* 宴会
blush [blʌʃ] *v.* 脸红，羞愧，呈现红色，使成红色
shade [ʃeid] *v.* 遮蔽，使阴暗，使渐变，微减

14

maple ['meip] *n.* 枫树
establishment [is'tæbkiʃmənt] *n.* 公共机构

15

gorgeous ['gɔːdʒəs] *adj.* 华丽的，灿烂的
fluster ['flʌstə] *v.* 慌慌张张的行动，混乱

16

independence [indi'pendəns] *n.* 独立，自主
community [kə'mjuniti] *n.* 公社，团体，
luxurious [lʌg'zjuəriəs] *adj.* 奢侈的，豪华的

17

washstand ['wɔʃstæmd] *n.* 盥洗盆，脸盆架
regardless [ri'gaːdlis] *adj.* 不管，不顾，不注意

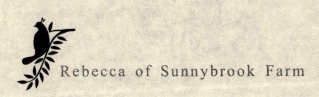

Rebecca of Sunnybrook Farm